BRITISH RAIL SCENE REMEMBERED

BRITISH RAIL SCENE REMEMBERED
MORE PHOTOGRAPHS FROM THE 1970s AND EARLY 1980s

ANDY SPARKS

The
History
Press

First published 2018

The History Press
97 St George's Place
Cheltenham
GL50 3QB
www.thehistorypress.co.uk

British Library Cataloguing in Publication Data.
A catalogue record for this book is available from the British Library.

ISBN 978 0 7509 8575 8

Typesetting and origination by The History Press
Printed and bound by Thomson Press, India

Frontispiece: **Arrivals and departures.** I have certain favourite platforms from which I like to watch trains coming and going. All those at Scarborough were close to the top of my favourites list during the 1970s and 1980s, it was amazing how much rail activity the seaside town generated. Loco-hauled excursions and timetabled trains were shoehorned in amongst the many DMU workings. It was a delight to stand close to the massive semaphore signal gantry and watch it all happening. In this shot, taken during mid-August 1975, 45014 *The Cheshire Regiment* is waiting to depart with a return Merrymaker excursion bound for Nottingham. The Eastern Region allocated Class 104 is arriving with a service train from Hull.

CONTENTS

INTRODUCTION

Welcome to *British Rail Scene Remembered*. It follows on from my previous tomes *British Rail Northern Scene*, *British Rail Northern Scene Coast to Coast* and *British Rail Scene*; all of which cover the gritty BR blue era of change, hope, neglect, modernisation, rationalisation and strife, using my photographs and words. The period of 1970s and early 1980s was a curious mix of great and not-so-great days. It was a fascinating and important time in railway history.

Fortunately, the books sold well, hence this fourth offering. I hope you find this one also hits the mark, then more will follow. I found it difficult to think of a title for this one: I could only come up with *British Rail Scene 2*, which really was a case of 'Andy shows promise, but could do better'. Amy and the team at History Press suggested swapping the '2' for 'Remembered' – I responded by saying 'Brilliant!' and wondered why I hadn't thought of that.

Remembered is a perfect title, because all of the captions are based on my memories. Once again, please excuse me if I have got some details wrong; forty years or so have elapsed since I took the photographs. I started taking all sorts of railway photographs in 1972 at the age of 14. I soon found that railways were, and still are, full to the brim with fantastic photo opportunities. I went all over the railway network: north, east, south and west. The world of Britain's railways really was my oyster. Looking back, I am now surprised how far I travelled and where I was allowed access to, my camera seemed to be a passport to lots of places that I had previously only dreamt of visiting. I continued my camerawork until 1982, when the likes of family commitments, love life, work and other distractions such as cars took hold. I have had a passion for railways since I was a small boy, but it didn't resurface until the late 1990s, triggered by a change in circumstances. I guess it's a similar story for many readers of this book. Over the ensuing years I kept most of my photographic work safe, but I did lose quite a few negatives, photographs, slides and un-processed films along the way – this was my fault. I have only myself to blame, and I am still beating myself up about it.

From that turning point at the end of the 1990s, I started to round up my photographs from the various places I had tucked them away. Negatives were printed/scanned, contact sheets scanned and unprocessed films processed (they came out well, despite being thirty years out of date). In addition, thanks to the wonders of modern day technology, I was also able to save previously un-saveable images using Microsoft Paint. Back in the 1970s I had a phase of developing films and then printing them using a darkroom at school and the box room at home. I got into a terrible mess: the negatives ended up chemically stained, scratched, under- or over-developed. Most of my prints also left a lot to be desired. Hence my need to resort to Paint and a lot of patience to put matters right. Hopefully, when you peruse this book, you won't be able to tell which photographs have had any special attention. It's a good job I didn't throw them in the bin all those years ago, I would have been beating myself up even more.

Once the rounding-up and rescuing mission was complete, I found I'd ended up with a vast portfolio of railway photographs, many of which hadn't been properly seen before by anyone, including me. I thought that I must do something constructive with them. Having to write a lot to obtain work-related qualifications and finding I liked it, I got it in my head I could pen a 'photo feature' article. I selected a few of my rediscovered photographs and memories then set about writing the article. The idea worked, it got published. Then I did it a few times more. After that came the book idea, and fortunately that worked too.

Now we are on book four. What's this one all about, you may ask. As previously, I have selected photographs from my bursting-at-the-seams portfolio to create five themed chapters: Arrivals, Between Duties, Places to Go & Things to Do, A Different Perspective and Inclement Weather. In all cases, I have tried my best to make the photographic content interesting and varied, and I hope my best is good enough. Each one starts with an introduction, while the photographs have comprehensive and informative captions, the writing of which I have really enjoyed doing. It was surprising how much I could remember when I peered into each one and how much I have learnt from double-checking things. The Internet and my stash of well-leafed Ian Allans and old timetables have helped a lot with this aspect. Amazingly, when looking at the photographs I can invariably remember the whole day of photo taking, such as how I'd got to places, what I saw, who I went with, why I'd gone, what went right and what went wrong. It's surprising how many memories one photograph can jog. I hope you enjoy the results.

For the passengers on board, a train drawing into a station marks a major or an intermediate stage in a journey. They may be about to get off, or could they be stopping on, travelling further? They might be enjoying the journey, or they might not be. They may be bored, excited, happy, upset or worried. They might be in a group, a couple or single, or possibly going to see a friend, lover or relation, or on their way home from seeing them. They could be going on holiday, to a sporting event, on a day trip, coming home from work, going to work, or on a shopping expedition. The possibilities are endless. If it was me, whatever my reason to travel, I'd feel sorry to be getting off. If I wasn't about to get off, the station stop would be marking down my minutes or hours of train ride enjoyment. I'd still sit on a train all day, if I could – sometimes, I do. A long train journey is to be relished.

The arrival might well be eagerly anticipated by passengers waiting for it on the platform, the precursor to a fantastic day out or holiday. It would certainly be a welcome sight for weary travellers heading home, especially homeward-bound workers. My 1960s family holidays and day trips to the seaside or one of our other favourite places, such as Buxton, meant boarding an incoming train. In the case of North Wales, it would mean climbing aboard a train at Manchester Exchange. It would be Black 5 or green-liveried Class 40 hauled, and the train would be made up of maroon BR and pre-Nationalisation coaches that arrived empty from Red Bank Carriage Sidings. If it wasn't empty stock, it would probably have started out from West Yorkshire – this meant a quick dash for an empty compartment. The anticipation and gradual build of excitement generated by the imminent arrival was immense, and this was compounded by garbled tannoy announcements and fellow passengers getting into position in readiness for the dash to climb aboard. You can imagine the fantastic sight and sound of the impressive, spine-tingling ensemble arriving, and how greatly accentuated it was by me being only three feet tall. The wonderful mixture of railway sounds, the smells, the hustle and bustle in a big mainline station all helped to cement my passion for trains – forever. My formative years were BR's transition period from steam to diesel/electric, but the period in railway history doesn't really matter with regard to the effect it has, apart from making

it our favourite. The arrival effect, I am sure, will apply to thousands of fellow railway enthusiasts. It is likely to be happening right now, be it on a preserved railway or a modern one anywhere in the world.

The arrival might be the end of a shift for the loco crew or guard. It might involve changeover from one form of traction to another prior to continuing the journey; in the case of 1970s Crewe, Anglo-Scottish Inter-City trains would swop from diesel to electric traction. My favourite swap over was to a Class 50 double header – fantastic. If the arrival meant the end of a journey at a terminus station, it would signal the opportunity to ask the driver of the incoming loco if I could cab it. I guess this would be frowned upon today in the case of a modern service train. I haven't tried asking lately.

For me, standing at the end of a platform simply watching trains arrive is brilliant. I loved doing it back in the 1970s and 1980s. I still do it now. Sadly, on the modern railway network it can be a rather lonely experience. Fellow platform end enthusiasts are not as plentiful as they used to be. Today it's much easier to know about delays, re-routing, loco or Multiple Unit usage thanks to the Internet and mobile phones – sadly, this takes away the element of surprise. During the 1970s and 1980s, old-fashioned word of mouth was the only way of knowing if something different or special was going to arrive. It was also a good way of finding out if something wasn't coming. This information was often supplied by a select few who, for some reason, were privy to the all-important gen. Did they get it from BR sources, or other members of the select few relaying it to each other? In my case, I tended to just turn up and wait, photographing anything and everything arriving. I am glad I did, as much of it is now history. Fortunately, fellow enthusiasts have saved quite a few of the locos, Multiple Units, coaches, van and wagons I photographed. Today we can enjoy watching them arrive on preserved railways and occasionally on the modern railway network, just as we did all those years ago. I take my hat off to all those enthusiasts, thank you.

The time has arrived to check out my first chapter's photographs and captions, I hope they don't disappoint. There are four to follow, I wouldn't want you to get off before the end of the book, unless you are just breaking up the journey.

Sunny Totnes. This is one of my favourite shots of all time. It captures everything that was so great about my carefree 1970s summer holidays in Devon – the sun was always shining, hardly a cloud in the sky, trains a-plenty, hauled by Westerns! Although the short reign of the Class 52 was almost at an end when I took this shot in mid-August 1976, they were still very much in evidence on the fast London Paddington Inter-City services to and from the South West. Here, 1072 *Western Glory* slowly draws into Totnes with a train from Plymouth. I was on a Youth Hostelling/Rail Rover holiday with a couple of mates; we took this train as far as Newton Abbot, where we took a Class 47 hauled train to Paignton. We were making our way to a hostel, which was hidden down a country lane between Paignton and Kingswear, close to the steam railway. Opposite was a small country club, which most hostellers frequented. It had a disco and plenty of cheap scrumpy that the proprietor collected from a farm in his rather tired Jensen Interceptor. The only problem was that the hostel's doors were locked soon after 10 p.m., and hangovers were no good when you had to do chores before leaving the morning after!

Arrival of the new order. An unidentified, newly drafted in from the North West of England, Class 50 arrives at Newton Abbot in October 1974, with a service from London Paddington. It looks rather odd without a nameplate – it wasn't until January 1978 that the class started to be named, with 50035 *Ark Royal* being the first. I bagged this shot from a BR excursion returning to Manchester. The loco was just about to pass 08646, which was kept busy shunting wagons and coaching stock at this still-busy rail hub. I had hung out of the window as my train passed through, hoping for a Western at the front of the train. At the time, I was disappointed to find it had been usurped by a Class 50, but it also told me that the mass withdrawal of the Class 52 was imminent. I knew that the North West was full of under-utilised 50s which had largely been made redundant after the West Coast Mainline Anglo-Scottish electrification had been completed; if they were all to be transferred to Western Region depots, the 52 was doomed. This told me I had to get cracking on photographing as many Westerns as possible before their withdrawal. What I didn't do, which I should have, was take photos of the final days of Class 50s in the North West, particularly when they were hauling Barrow-in-Furness passenger trains along the coast from Carnforth.

The Devonian. Early style split headcode box 45013 sweeps into Newton Abbot during the summer of 1974 with *The Devonian*, its Paignton-bound train from Bradford – doesn't the name sound splendid? It's great that there are still some trains that have names – *The Cathedrals Express*, *Caledonian Sleeper* and *Torbay Express* spring to mind. I think the more the better, I'm sure passengers would be rather taken with the idea. I think 1974 was the first year that *The Devonian* didn't have full dining car facilities, another lamented throwback to bygone days.

Eastern becomes Western. Despite it being several years since Eastern Region Class 31s had replaced the short-lived Hymek Class 35 mixed traffic locos on the Western Region, the sight of one pulling into Paddington looked wrong to me. Here, 31135 arrives with empty coaching stock from its home depot's (Old Oak Common) carriage sidings, during May 1980. The loco had previously been allocated to East Anglia's March depot. In later years, it became part of the modern railway's Departmental Fleet and was painted a rather undignified yellow. It was withdrawn in April 2000 after almost thirty years' service, far longer than the Hymeks' average ten. I had made my way to Brunel's glorious Central London station in search of Class 50s, by then, their presence was diminished, having been usurped by Class 253 Inter-City 125 HSTs. Ironically, just a few years earlier, enthusiasts had flocked to Paddington in search of the dwindling numbers of Class 52 Westerns, which were quickly being replaced by 50s. A few months after I took this photo, I made Waterloo and Clapham Junction 'must-do' locations for 50 haulage photos.

Deltic arrival. Mighty 55014 *The Duke of Wellington's Regiment* arrives at Kings Cross on 21 April 1979 with 1A08, 06.12 from Newcastle Central. I had a little bit of time to get into position in readiness for this photograph, because I was forewarned of its imminent arrival by the loco's mighty Napier engines, which could clearly be heard being put to good use inside the Gasworks Tunnel. There was lots of glorious noise, accompanied by a goodly amount of clag as it hauled its lengthy train up the gradient into the station. Amazingly, Kings Cross is still a great location to take Deltic photographs – occasionally a beautifully preserved example hauls a charter train to or from the station. This would have been hard to believe when they were being withdrawn from BR service during the early 1980s.

Boat train arrival. This photo was taken during the summer of 1981, just before many of the Southern Region's express passenger service EMUs' classy blue and grey livery was replaced by the odd-looking 'Jaffa Cake' colouring. Fortunately, the rather snazzy Network South East livery soon corrected BR's livery choice aberration. In this photo, a refurbished 4 CEP/Class 411 EMU, experimentally numbered 411512 (previously 7119) arrives at London Victoria with a boat train from Folkestone Harbour. I guess the trialling of this method of identification was in-keeping with the by then established way of numbering EMUs on other regions, but it was to be short-lived, as this unit was soon renumbered in the Southern four-digit style, becoming 1512. Whilst only seven coaches are in evidence in this shot, the train may well have been made up of three Class 411s coupled together, making up a twelve-coach train. These boat trains became a thing of the past when the Channel Tunnel opened, which also resulted in the closure of quirky Folkestone Harbour and Dover's very impressive Western Docks station. Incidentally, the EMU in the foreground is Class 423/4VEP number 7891.

Southern suburban personified. The vestiges of the old Southern Railway abound in this photograph. To complete the scene, it could really do with green enamel signs and matching liveried train. How many things can you see that the modern-day railway preservationist/railwayana collector would probably go mad for? Bullied-design-influenced Class 415.1/4EPB number 5109 arrives at Clapham Junction with a service from London Bridge. By the looks of the waiting passengers, nobody wants to join this train – it's odds on that a few were about to get off though.

White DMU. In the gritty environment of late 1970s/early 1980s British Rail, the largely white livery being applied to DMUs wasn't very practical; it didn't take long for them to look dirty. This didn't help BR's endeavours to rid itself of the grubby, down-at-heel steam age past that many members of the public still associated with it. During the summer of 1980, Class 116, headed up by M51151, draws into Leicester – it's the 16.37 second-class-only service to Birmingham New Street. Check out the superb array of semaphore signalling, Midland Railway signal box and the Class 08, 25s and 31 stabled within the neat-looking depot.

Footex 20s. On a wonderfully lit Saturday in late August 1980, a pair of Class 20s, fronted by 20046, arrive at Nottingham with an early season football special, full of supporters coming to the city to watch their away match. I can't remember where the train was from, but I am sure an avid Nottingham fan will be able to determine what team was playing against them around that time. I presume the train hadn't come far because twenty hauled passenger trains were a rarity beyond the confines of the East Midlands railway network – unless, of course, the locos had replaced another form of motive power en route from somewhere further afield.

Class 25 double header. 25133 heads up a fine pairing of Class 25s hauling their train from Skegness into a timewarped and desolate-looking Boston station, during August 1980. If my memory serves me correctly, it is bound for Stoke-on-Trent, but it is a stopping service train rather than an excursion, so I may be wrong. The locos might well have been filling in for the usual Class 20 pairings used on summer season Skegness 'bucket-and-spade trains' to/from Derby and Nottingham. I was on an East Midlands Rail Rover, which I squeezed every drop of goodness out of. Its western extremity covered New Mills Central, a few stations away from my home station Reddish North, so it was a brilliant buy. I think something similar is available today, so one day my 1980 steps might be retraced, but I know it won't be the same. For sure, the Skegness line is now a shadow of its former self.

Stoke Poly. The building in the background is Stoke-on-Trent Polytechnic – remember polytechnics? They were very 1960/70s, and most cities had them. During the 1990s they became universities and Stoke is now part of Staffordshire University, which has places of learning in several parts of the county. The Class 310 EMU number 060, arriving with an all-stations-stopping train from Manchester Piccadilly adds to the 1960/70s scene. I liked these superbly designed units; both their interior and exterior epitomised the period. Sadly, their 1980s refurbishment resulted in them acquiring flat windscreens and different interiors, and I didn't like them as much after that. It was quite unusual to have a 310 deployed on this service, normally a Class 304 would have been used. At the time, they'd be used on semi-fast and fast services serving major London Midland Region stations such as Birmingham New Street, London Euston and Manchester Piccadilly.

Crewe 87. It's October 1974 and this Class 87 is just six months old. 87022 is arriving at Crewe with a fast Manchester Piccadilly to London Euston service. Since the mid-1960s this service was the preserve of the Class 86, however 81s and 85s weren't uncommon. After the introduction of the 87s, this wasn't the case. This loco was named *Cock o' the North* on 30 June 1978, then renamed *Lew Adams the Black Prince* from 1995–2004, and then it reverted back to *Cock o' the North* between 2006 and 2007. The Class 87s were displaced by the introduction of Virgin Pendolinos on their stomping ground, the West Coast Mainline, but being very usable locos, quite a few were sold to the Bulgarian Railways, including 87022. During 2013, the loco caught fire whilst hauling a freight train and, at the time of writing this caption, I couldn't find out if had been repaired, rebuilt or scrapped after the fire.

Class 40 arrival. Crewe has been associated with Class 40s ever since their late 1950s introduction, replacing steam on the West Coast Mainline, until their early 1980s demise. Even after that, four withdrawn examples (40012, 40060, 40118 and 40135) were resurrected during 1985 to help with station's remodelling project. It was intended that they'd only be used for a month, but this wasn't the case, and they went on to haul a wide variety of trains. The last of the four, 40060, was withdrawn in March 1987. 40012, 40118 and 40135 were subsequently preserved. In this shot, taken in August 1975, an unidentified 40 arrives with a relief train working from Blackpool, which terminated at Crewe. During the summer, it was quite common for BR to supplement their 'Saturday Only' timetabled trains with relief trains, particularly those servicing popular seaside destinations. This one would have provided a useful additional feeder service to East/West Midlands, West Coast Mainline and Welsh trains.

Manchester Victoria. During the summer of 1974, a pair of Class 504 two-car sets arrive at Manchester Victoria. At this time, these EMUs still carried head codes, as can be seen on leading unit M77181. The train to the left is a short parcels working that is formed of ex-LMS full brake coaches; it's bound for Oldham Mumps Parcels Depot, hauled by a Skin Head Class 24. Amazingly, its journey only started from one of Manchester Victoria's bay platforms – surely a van journey along Oldham Road would have been more cost effective? Of course, it was, and this operation did eventually bite the dust.

Newcastle–Liverpool train. With its new flat nose, 45129 descends Miles Platting Bank into Manchester Victoria, hauling the every-other-hour service from Newcastle to Liverpool Lime Street. From the mid-1970s, Peak Class 45s and 46s lost their headcode panel front ends in favour of the headlamp fitted type sported by this loco. I remember going to the Derby Works Open Day in 1976, where I saw several new front ends stacked up and waiting to be fitted to Peaks coming in for attention. This shot was taken during the summer of 1977, when the beautiful looking Class 124 Trans-Pennine DMUs still operated the Liverpool Lime Street to Hull via York service; they ran between the hours when the Newcastle train didn't run. By the end of the decade, this service had been replaced by one serving York and Scarborough, more often than not hauled by Class 40s. These trains became very popular with 40 bashers. The 124s were transferred to services serving Manchester Piccadilly, Hull, and Cleethorpes, via Sheffield.

High-speed 506. In this photo, I have inadvertently made it look like this Class 506 is doing about 100mph as it approaches the Ashburys station stop. In fact, it was probably only doing about 20mph, I had got my shutter speed wrong. At the time, summer 1978, the station and its surroundings were still very much how it had been since Victorian times. Ashburys was at the centre of the Gorton/Openshaw industrial area, where there were massive engineering factories providing employment for thousands of people, including Manchester Steel, Johnson and Nephew and Crossley Engines. Sadly, they have all long since closed. Other well-known local notables had closed during 1960s, which gave an early indication of what the future held for the area – those that closed during the '60s included Beyer Peacock, BR Gorton Works and Armstrong Whitworth. Imagine how many people had trudged up and down the steps leading to the road beneath the station over the years. You can see the steps at the bottom-left of the photo.

Bangor disappointment. I patiently waited for ages at the Holyhead end of Bangor station for a Manchester Victoria-bound loco-hauled passenger train to appear. Instead, on this overcast summer 1973 afternoon, a Class 105 Cravens DMU arrived instead. You can imagine my disappointment, if it had been loco-hauled I would have been treated to the delights of either Class 24, 25, 40 or 47 power at the front of the train. Of course, nowadays, I wouldn't be disappointed – I'd love a run along the North Wales Coast in a 105. Thank goodness one two-car set has been preserved.

Going the wrong way. The destination blind on this Carlisle-based 2x2-car Class 108 train gives the impression it is bound for Whitehaven, but it has probably come from there. Hopefully it didn't mislead any passengers intending to go to the fishing and coal-mining town. It's arriving at Arnside station during Easter 1974, bound for Lancaster. The 108s were the mainstay for the circuitous, but highly picturesque, coastal route from Carnforth to Carlisle. This remained the case until Second Generation DMUs took over during the 1980s. The only thing that spoilt them was the three bars across the slam door droplights, making window hanging nigh on impossible, and they gave me the impression I was in a cage. I guess some people might say that's the best place for me.

Penistone 110. Class 110 DMUs were known as Calder Valley Units, because they plied the Trans-Pennine line passing through that area of West Yorkshire; the route being between Manchester Victoria and Bradford/Leeds, via Rochdale, Todmorden, Hebden Bridge and Halifax. They were more powerful versions of the Class 104 and had a fancy front end. They were allocated to Bradford Hammerton Street, which meant they were often deployed on other West Yorkshire services, in particular Leeds to Morecambe. However, on the occasion of my photograph, taken during March 1980, this example has strayed into South Yorkshire, and it is arriving at Penistone on a Sheffield–Huddersfield service. This route proved to be popular in the late 1970s and early 1980s for Class 76 Woodhead Electric rail fans. Penistone was the place to alight to witness lots of 76 activity – that's why I'd got myself there. Although, I must admit I drove across the Pennines from Manchester in my beat-up VW Beetle, instead of going by train.

Doncaster panorama. The road bridge spanning the northern approach to Doncaster station was perfect for watching the station's comings and goings. In this August 1979 photo, Inter-City 125 HST 254 022 is snaking its way into Platform 1 with a London Kings Cross-bound service. Visible on the northbound platforms is a Class 55 hauled London to York train, which has also just arrived. To the far right are the busy sidings and BREL workshops. The HSTs have proved to be a really good investment for BR, being used on the East Coast Mainline long after its electrification and de-nationalisation.

The esplanade. A couple of the Isle of Wight line's superbly vintage 1927-built ex-London Underground Class 486 EMUs, headed up by number 035. They have just arrived at the grandly named Ryde Esplanade station. It was a brilliant idea to use redundant tube stock on the island's truncated railway, it was a low-cost solution to keeping the line open after steam came to an end and the railway network was cut back during 1966. This service is bound for Ryde's Pier Head loaded with passengers who will soon afterwards take the ferry to Portsmouth. Passengers can be seen making their way to waiting Southern Vectis buses, along with others queuing for different bus services. They have just arrived on a train from Pier Head, and are probably incoming holidaymakers heading for towns and resorts no longer served by the railway. I took this photograph one Saturday afternoon in May 1976.

Doomed Gateshead. A refurbished Class 101 DMU arrives at Gateshead station in May 1980. It's not going to Newcastle, despite the destination blind saying it is. The driver looks like he's just let on to the two chaps walking along the wooden platform, he certainly appears to be enjoying his work. The station's well-cared-for appearance doesn't give any indication that just one year later it would be closed. The whole place has since been demolished and now there is little trace of it.

10.37 arrival at Carlisle. It was late morning on 20 April 1977 when I captured on FP4 film 86240 arriving with the 09.05 from Glasgow Central to London Euston. The train is due out of Carlisle at 10.37, so passengers will have to be quick getting on and off the train – they do look like they have been standing around for a while awaiting its arrival. In the centre road, a Travelling Post Office (TPO) coach can be seen. 86240 was named *Bishop Eric Treacy* on 3 April 1979 at Penrith station in memory of the recently passed away master railway photographer. The loco was withdrawn during October 2002 and then scrapped at Rotherham in April 2005.

Push pull Edinburgh. A rather worse for wear 27106 lifts its train from the tunnel beneath the Scottish National Gallery and Princess Street Gardens. It's December 1974 and there is some frost on the sleepers. This arrival at Edinburgh Waverley is from Glasgow Queen Street; this service was quite novel, utilising a Class 27 loco at each end of a rake of Mark 2 coaches. This is now commonly known as top and tailing and quite often undertaken on preserved railways. However, unlike on preserved lines, these trains ran intensively at high speed (up to 90mph) throughout the week – no wonder this loco looks a bit dishevelled. This method of operation was a great success and was the forerunner of the equally successful Class 47/7 powered Push-Pull Glasgow-Edinburgh/Aberdeen services that replaced it in 1980. Unlike many other class members, 27106 didn't get scrapped, it has been preserved and beautifully restored.

Early morning at Culrain. Whilst on a youth hostelling holiday with two of my mates during August 1981, we stopped the night at SYHA's astonishing and rather impressive Carbisdale Castle. It's located a short distance from the Far North line's Culrain station. It was the last castle to be built in Scotland, dating to 1905, sumptuously furnished in stately home style, and this is how it largely remained, including life-sized statues of naked ladies – most distracting for a clean-living railway enthusiast! After more than 60 years as a youth hostel, it closed in 2011, needing a lot of repairs and, at the time of writing this caption, it was up for sale. Anyway, we were on our way to the Orkneys and we needed to leave early to catch the first train of the day to Thurso. This photo shows it arriving at 08.04 (06.15 ex-Inverness) hauled by one of the Inverness-allocated Class 37s, previously based at Stratford depot in London.

2 BETWEEN DUTIES

Like many readers of this book, whenever I'm within sight of a railway, its depots, sidings and stations, I scan the scene looking for things of interest – locos, DMU/EMUs and trains awaiting their next duty quite often catch our eye. Sometimes their appearance is unexpected, sometimes not. Whatever the case, generally it's a 'here today gone tomorrow' scene – almost instant history – when they have headed off to fulfil their next duties. They are certain to be history one day and often lamented when the subjects of our attention have long since been withdrawn from service.

I still peer through carriage windows and stand on platforms to catch sight of between duties scenes. In addition, I am guilty of driving along looking across at sidings and depots. My local Longsight Depot is a prime example; it runs parallel to the A57. On the rare occasion that I am on a bus I do the same.

Back in the 1970s and '80s, it was much easier than now to photograph these scenes. Free access to most depots, sidings and stabling points provided endless photo opportunities, but that's not the case nowadays – health and safety rules, along with high security, have put an end to this. In addition to easy access back then, virtually every train had droplight windows, which could be lowered in readiness for passing known places where between duties shots could be grabbed. Once prepared, I'd have my camera ready to photograph whatever was present. Leaning out of the train wasn't necessary, just a scratch-, smear- and reflection-free view. It's now rarely possible with the widespread use of hermetically sealed modern trains – very frustrating. This shot-grabbing technique was ideal when on a train that was taking me into areas I didn't usually frequent, and dangerous lineside locations could be photographed without being in danger.

Looking back at the things and places I photographed, it is surprising – or maybe it isn't – how much has changed. Gone are many of the places I made a beeline for in order to bag additional between-duties photographs. The likes of Buxton Depot, Guide Bridge Stabling Point, Newton Abbot Depot, Llandudno Junction Carriage Sidings, Manchester Victoria centre roads, Reddish Depot and York Yard are now no more. They are a fading memory; if you didn't know that they had existed, it would be hard to believe they ever did. They have succumbed to dereliction, Mother Nature, redevelopment and modernisation. I sometimes stand in places where I used to photograph locos and DMUs waiting their next duties, feeling a bit sad and old. At Llandudno Junction and Newton Abbot, for example, I now look out on overgrown tracks, shrubs, trees and fast food outlets.

On the up-side, quite a few of my past haunts are still going strong – better still, some house-operational, revenue-earning First Generation locomotives. It would have been hard to imagine, forty years ago, that already aging motive power would still be in use today. Prime examples are Class 08, 20, 37, 47 and 73s; whilst not in plentiful supply, they are still there if you can spot them, rubbing shoulders with modern locos, stabled in depots and sidings between their duties. One of the best places to currently witness this phenomenon is Carlisle Kingmoor Depot and Yard. The only problem is that I can no longer grab a shot from a passing service train and a casual walkabout, without permission, is a total no-no.

From this selection of photographs there's a lot of between-duties places that remain and lots that don't. The reasons for their existence have long since gone, been changed or have been reduced. Many locos, multiple units and rolling stock have long since been withdrawn, others haven't. Have a good look around.

Scorching hot Newton Abbot. In the baking hot sun, Plymouth's Laira-depot-allocated 47031 and an unidentified Class 52 Western await their next duties at Newton Abbot. They are in the loco depot sidings alongside the station. It's August 1974 and there is plenty of loco-hauled traffic to keep them busy, they won't be idle for long. It's odds-on that the Western's next duty will be a Paignton–London Paddington Inter-City service, while the 47 could have been next assigned to West of England Mainline freight, passenger, parcels, Motorail or permanent way working, all of which used motive power stabled at Newton Abbot. Check out the Western Region brown enamel running-in board, it wouldn't be there much longer: the station's matching totem signs had been replaced a few months earlier.

Southern in a GWR yard. When I took this photograph in late July 1973, it was less than ten years since diesel hydraulic locos replaced steam on the Western Region. This yard alongside Exeter St Davids station is still full of steam age remnants, including a water crane complete with a solid fuel burner water heater to stop it freezing. Even more poignant, it was only seven years since Southern Region steam and its matching green coaches had become a thing of the past. In this yard stands, slightly incongruously, Southern Region's new order Class 33, number 6546 (33028) with a rake of blue- and grey-liveried SR Mark 1 coaches. It had arrived on a service from London Waterloo earlier in the afternoon and would return during the early evening. In order to not block the station's platform, the consist was held in the yard until nearer the scheduled departure time. Incidentally, this loco was modelled by Graham Farish in N gauge as 33028.

Laira 46. Usually allocated to Cross-Country Inter-Regional passenger workings, Laira-allocated 46006 waits its next duty at what I think is Taunton, I am far from sure. There's a possibility it has hauled the mixed freight train, seen in the background, and is now waiting to return to Plymouth. Alternatively, it might be about to be moved into position in order to couple up to it. I am probably wrong on both counts, but someone out there might have the answer. The photograph was taken during September 1977 when old-style freight trains, such as the one shown in this photograph, were still keeping goods yards and locos busy.

Western Thunderbird. It's July 1974 at Bristol and 1025 *Western Guardsman* has just arrived at the outer reaches of Bath Road depot with three dead Class 47s in tow. To me, it didn't look like the 47s were available for duty, I guessed that they probably required remedial work at the well-equipped modern diesel depot. Alternatively, I reckoned that this was a serviceable loco move from another depot, with the 47s being intended to supplement Bath Road's loco allocation. Summer loco-hauled passenger workings on the Western Region's routes radiating from Bristol put a big strain the depot's available motive power. They would have been handy to have on the books. Whatever the case, Class 52 fans will no doubt wholeheartedly approve that a Western was used for the task of hauling dead 47s.

In the depths of South Wales. Awaiting their next duties are Laira's tired-looking and battle-scarred 37190, a Class 08 and another of the Western Region's fleet of trusty 37s. This photo was taken at Pantyffynnon on the Central Wales line on 19 February 1976. This was the junction for lines serving the National Coal Board's (NCB) Wernos Washery, Betws Drift, Abernant Colliery and Gwaun-Cae-Gurwen Colliery. The 37s were waiting their next turn of duty, taking loaded coal trains to distribution depots, factories and power stations on the Western Region network, while the 08 would have been engaged shunting wagons and serving the Washery. It was a Saturday afternoon, so the locos wouldn't be needed until the Monday when the pits got underway producing more wagon-loads of coal. The nose-mounted headlight on 37190 would have been a great asset to the driver when working in dimly lit or dark sidings and threading trains along dark rural freight lines. Many of lines serving collieries didn't have the best permanent way, being stubs of long-closed passenger routes, meaning the driver would have had to keep an extra close eye on the line ahead. In addition, locals walking on the track using it as a short cut, straying farm animals, fallen trees, landslides, rubbish and motor vehicles on unmanned level crossings were typical hazards. 37190 has been preserved and now looks far better now than it did in 1976.

Sunday afternoon at Ashford. On a sunny Sunday afternoon in July 1974, a pair of Class 423/4VEP EMUs headed up by 7875 waits in sidings alongside Ashford station for their next duties. The headcode blinds are blank – unlike other regions, the Southern used them for many years after the 1970s – and so they do not give us an indication of what their jobs will be next. The following morning rush hour will no doubt require them to be switched on early. A London Charing-Cross-bound service was the most likely first job of the day, or, alternatively, the units might have been moved to Dover or Ramsgate in readiness for the commuter rush to the Capital. Either way, the 423s would have had a busy week ahead of them.

Ashford station, its environs and trains changed considerably with the opening of the Channel Tunnel, twenty years after I took this photograph. It was expanded and renamed Ashford International. Eurostar trains destined for Brussels Midi, French Alps, Marseille, Paris Disneyland and Paris Nord now regularly call at the station. London Charing Cross, Victoria and South Coast services also call at the station, as well as a high speed service to and from London St Pancras. Unfortunately, the handsome looking Class 423s have long since been consigned to the scrap yard.

Overlooked by maisonettes. The occupants of the upper floors of these council-owned maisonettes would have had a good view of the railway and locos stabled below – I wonder if any of them became avid rail enthusiasts? I bet some did. The location is Vauxhall and Duddeston, 2 miles from Birmingham New Street on the Aston line, where there was a carriage sidings. It's a quiet August Bank Holiday Sunday in 1974, and awaiting their next duties (probably an empty coaching stock move into New Street) are 83001, 83014, Roarer 85027 and an almost out of sight Class 82. I well remember sneaking into Bury Depot during 1970 and seeing lines of original condition Class 82, 83 and 84 locos in store there. They looked fantastic with their electric blue liveries, small yellow warning panel front ends, cast lion and wheel bodyside emblems. To complete the package, they carried their cast E3XXX polished metal cab side numbers. I couldn't believe it. Although less than 10 years old, they were in store awaiting their fate – troublesome electrical systems and lack of work had meant mothballing was the only option. However, the electrification of the West Coast Mainline north of Crewe in 1974 required a lot more electric locos, and this led to them being taken out of store for refurbishment. Afterwards, they did see quite a bit of use throughout the West Coast Mainline's electrified network, but always seemed to be the underdog to Class 81, 85, 86 and 87 locos.

Beneath the castle ramparts. Back in the 1970s, Shrewsbury station and its approach lines were amazing. An unaffected-by-time and change mix of LMS and GWR, Shrewsbury was a superbly appointed station with a castle-like frontage, canopies and a fully functioning track layout that were a joy to behold. It was complemented by massive signal boxes and plenty of semaphores, both upper and lower quadrant varieties, and the signal arms were clearly regularly polished, so they gleamed in the sunlight. What's more amazing is that, at the time of writing forty years later, it remains very much the same. The well-cared-for vintage signalling is a joy to behold.

I took this photograph, with Shrewsbury Castle overlooking the scene, on 2 October 1976. I'd travelled to the city to photograph 6201 *Princess Elizabeth* hauling a steam special but, being more interested in modern traction, I just had to photograph 08220 and 08123 stabled in one of the station's bay platforms. Fortunately, like 6201, both locos were preserved when withdrawn from BR service. Weekends were a quiet time for the 08s, which were outstationed from Crewe Depot. Weekdays were a different matter as freights, parcel vans, coaching stock and permanent way shunts all needed their services. In addition, on other occasions I saw flat wagons with Vale of Rheidol Railway rolling stock on board, shunted into this particular bay by one of them. At the time, BR owned the steam-hauled narrow-gauge railway and overhauled its stock at BREL Swindon works, transferring it to and from Aberystwyth by rail.

Wolverhampton layover. I bagged this shot of 25104 on the approaches to Wolverhampton High Level station during February 1975 while it was on stand-by duty. At the time, it was allocated to Bescot Depot after a short spell at Sheffield's Tinsley Depot, but it spent just six months allocated to the busy West Midlands depot, due to a motive power shortage. For virtually all of its life the loco was based in the North West; after Bescot, it was allocated to Manchester's Longsight Depot, where it remained until its withdrawal in September 1982. It was cut up at BREL Swindon Works on New Year's Eve 1986.

East Midlands loco, through and through. This photo of 20156 and several other East Midlands allocated 20s was taken at Derby Works during its Open Day on 4 September 1976. It appeared to be in for some light work, although I might be wrong. It wouldn't be long before it would be doing what it was designed for.

The Class 20, one of English Electric's many success stories, was synonymous with the East Midlands. It was principally engaged in hauling freight (largely Derbyshire- and Nottinghamshire-mined coal), and feeding hungry power stations but passenger workings, such as the ever-popular Skegness services during the summer, were also one of their specialities. These trains' popularity were not just down to day trippers; 20 bashers, of which I was one, also ensured plenty of bums on seats. 20156, along with lots of other 20s, was allocated to Toton Depot until 1981 when, for some reason, it was singled out for transfer to Glasgow's Eastfield Depot. Unlike other class members, it didn't have a long life; it was withdrawn in July 1991 and then scrapped at MC Metals in Glasgow two years later. It still lives on though; it is possible to buy a Bachmann 00 gauge model of it in Railfreight grey and yellow livery.

East Holmes. On a brightly lit day during August 1980, 31180 crosses the swing bridge at Brayford Pool on its way to nearby Lincoln depot, where it would wait for its next job. The loco was based at Immingham for use mainly on freight-haulage work throughout Lincolnshire and beyond. In the Lincoln area, there were still quite a few rail-connected industrial concerns to generate work for it and its stable mates, including British Sugar at Bardney, GKN, Ley's, Shell at Torksey, and Lincoln coal yard and goods depot. East Holmes signal box, dating from 1873, remained in use until September 2008. It is a Grade II Listed Building, which hopefully will ensure the Victorian gem's survival. The 1869-built swing bridge is now a fixed structure. The loco depot closed during the late 1980s, and the site and its surroundings are now part of the city's university complex – including a large entertainment venue named 'The Engine Shed', which is a very modern building, unlike the depot 31180 was heading to.

Llandudno Junction trio. This shot was taken in the Junction's run-down, but fantastic to visit, Carriage Sidings and Depot complex during March 1978. It doubled up as a loco servicing depot/stabling point after the ex-steam-shed had been demolished in 1966. On hand, ready for their next duties, are the depot's trusty 08, a Class 40 that was the focus of many a North Wales coastline basher's attention and a Class 25. The 25s were often used to haul the Trawsfynydd Power Station nuclear flask trains and Associated Octel Amlych tank wagons. This wonderful place that I visited many times, bit the dust in 2000; now there's a KFC, McDonalds and a cinema in its place. You can surely guess where I'd rather go.

Day trip to Chester. Cravens Class 105s were common-place at Chester Depot when I took this photo during the summer of 1976. However, what was far from common was one of the Eastern Region examples; this two-car set in the foreground is headed up by E56435, which was allocated to Hull Botanic Gardens Depot. There being no through DMU service from the East Coast to Chester at the time, it's odds-on that it arrived on a BR day excursion working. The interloper would return later in the day. The opulent in comparison Class 120, standing further back in the servicing siding, would later on in the day be used on a Wrexham or Birkenhead line service.

Old and new order. Birkenhead EMU depot hosts Merseyside's old and new order on this September day in 1979. On the far right is newly built 507003, which formed part of a large fleet of 507s and 508s that would soon replace Merseyrail's vintage EMUs. The ex-LMS Class 502s and ex-LMS/early BR 503s. No doubt 507003 would soon be leaving the depot to be out and about on the Merseyrail network. The Class 502 number M28354M was also ready to leave after repairs; it spent its operational days working the network's Liverpool–Southport and Ormskirk services. Being unsuitable for running through BR's Mersey tunnel, it had to be towed by a diesel loco the long way around to Liverpool before resuming revenue-earning duties. The last surviving 502s were withdrawn from passenger service in 1980, but M28354M was then renumbered ADB977017 and used with M28357M (ADB977018) as a departmental train based at Kirkdale. They lasted until 1986.

24s at Arpley. The two variations of the Class 24 – Skin Head (no roof headcode panel) 5063 (24063), still in original green livery; and the later-built 5137 (24137), with roof headcode panel – await their next duties at Warrington's Arpley Yard. It's Christmas 1974 and there's little need for these Crewe-allocated mixed-traffic locos. Once the festivities were over they would be back in use hauling trains. Arpley was a once a busy stabling point for locos used on the area's freight trains, many of which used the route via Lymm and Apethorn Junction to Godley Junction, hauling trains to and from the Woodhead route. Curiously, the Skin Heads tended to last longer, and this applied to these two 24s. 24063 was withdrawn in April 1979, 24137 was history by July 1976.

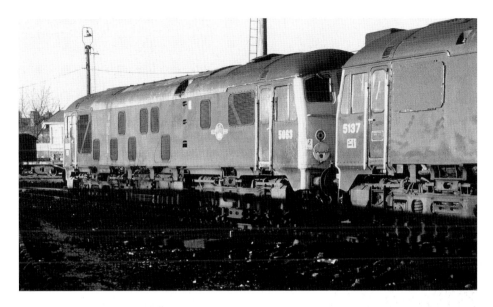

Longsight haunt. Of all the BR Depots that I visited during the 1970s and 80s, Longsight was my second-most frequent haunt (Reddish came first). I usually gained unofficial access through the big gates just off Hyde Road. On my earlier visits, I would pass terraced houses that overlooked the entrance, but these were later demolished as part of Manchester's slum clearance programme. In one of them lived the nearby Belle Vue Amusement and Zoo Park's Flea Circus. The circus was an amazing sight to behold – apparently, only human fleas could perform the death-defying feats.

After walking through the diesel area of the depot, I would reach the electric loco section. I was never disappointed, there were always locos to see. On this occasion, one Saturday afternoon during February 1979, standing amongst cast-off materials and overlooking Kirkmanshulme Lane are Glasgow Shields Road allocated 81017, along with an unidentified Class 86. They didn't stop long at the depot, being constantly required to haul trains. Their tasks included Inter-City passenger services, Freightliner trains from the adjacent BR Container Terminal and van workings serving Mayfield Parcel Depot – the long forgotten and derelict station standing alongside Piccadilly.

Lazy afternoon. Unlike nowadays, Manchester Piccadilly had long periods of inactivity on Sundays during the 1970s. This photo, taken in 1976, is a good example of how it was. The Class 40 is stabled in the area where Post Office road vehicles would arrive to load up and collect the contents of parcels trains. The open road enabled vehicles and train spotters/enthusiasts to easily gain access to the station's platform – there was no need to buy a platform ticket, which was very handy when funds were low. At night, the lazy Sunday scene would change considerably when the parcels and newspaper train activity got underway and that is what this Class 40 was waiting for.

The perfect photo. This was one of the first photographs I took with my brand new Zorki 4 camera that my mum and dad bought for me as an early birthday present in 1973. I was really pleased, and still am, with this shot of Willesden Depot's E3105 (86030) at Manchester Piccadilly. The loco is running out of the station after being released from the platform it arrived at, hauling an Inter-City service from London Euston. Prior to this move, another Class 86 would have coupled up to the coaching stock and taken it back to Euston on a returning service. E3105 would have waited amongst the complicated sprawl of lines outside the station for the next service to arrive from London, it would then have coupled up to the rear coach in readiness to return the train to the capital. E3105 might well have done this several times in one day.

Ready for night duties. Taken from Guide Bridge's lengthy footbridge on a September 1979 evening, this photo shows how busy Guide Bridge Stabling Point was back then. I can see seven Class 76s, a 47 and four 40s, all ready for action to haul night freights radiating from Ardwick, Ashburys, Dewsnap sidings, Guide Bridge and Godley Junction. The pair of 76s in the foreground have just arrived with the coal train on the far left; they have brought it over Woodhead from a South Yorkshire mine. The 47 coming off the stabling point will couple up to the train and take it onwards to a North-West power station. Happy days, hours of free entertainment.

The mighty forty. Ever since I was a young lad I have been mad keen on Class 40s. I am now on my second stint as editor of the Class 40 Preservation Society's magazine *The Whistler*. I first remember them racing along the North Wales Coast line at Pensarn, in green livery with a rake of maroon coaches in tow – an awesome sight. Being a Manchester enthusiast of a certain age, they were for many years an everyday sight and sound. Despite this, I never tired of them.

I took this shot of 371 (40171) entering Guide Bridge Stabling Point in October 1973. I can almost hear its distinctive whistling sound and see the shadow of the bridge moving as it rumbled away from me. The loco had just come off the Denton line running light engine. It is a Saturday morning, so it's likely the loco will have to wait until Monday before resuming haulage duties.

Pussy willows. This spring 1979 shot was taken alongside the entrance to Reddish Depot, which was amidst a sprawling Manchester Corporation housing estate. I was first taken there by my mum and dad when I was little; it was a nice walk from home and passed a family friend's horse that was stabled on Station Road. My earliest memories of the depot are of the stunning blue-liveried Midland Pullman trains that were serviced there, along with EM1 (Class 76) and EM2 (Class 77) locos with unreadable names – at five the words were too big and complicated for me. The Class 47 shown in this photo will soon head off along the Fallowfield line towards Gorton or Guide Bridge. Although primarily built to service Woodhead DC electric locos and Class 506s, diesels often delivered a surprising variety of locos and EMUs for attention. For example, it was commonplace to see Class 304, 310, 502 and 503s there. Lots of diesel traction, including 08, 24s, 25s, 40s, 47s and 50s, made their own way there to have work undertaken. Its spacious and clean working environment, skilled workforce, wheel-turning machine, heavy lift cranes and jacks in effect made it an annexe to BREL Crewe Works. Sadly, my favourite depot is all gone now, and a housing estate now stands on the sprawling site.

On standby. This Healey Mills allocated Class 40 is whistling away nicely in the winter sun at Huddersfield in 1978. The loco is on standby duty at the town's station and is strategically located for the routes radiating from this hub including, those serving Penistone, Standedge Tunnel/Stalybridge, Leeds, and Wakefield. Piloting and failed loco rescue would have been amongst its duties. At the time Healey Mills was an awesome place, comprising a massive depot and goods yard. The first time I saw it was whilst visiting a customer at the nearby Procor wagon works – I was amazed. I can still remember the buyer there used to give me a really good earbashing for late deliveries. He must have liked me, though – or what the company I worked for made – because he kept giving us purchase orders. Unfortunately, despite passing Healey Mills many times whilst visiting him, I never once took a photo of the yards. My loss. It's still there, but a derelict shadow of its former self.

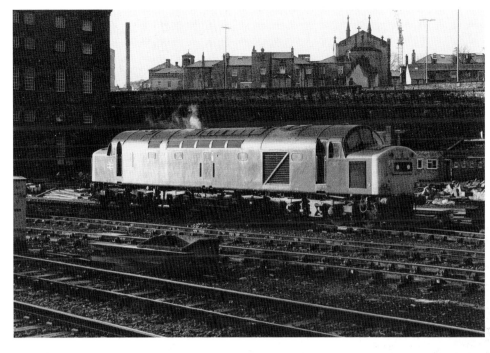

Tired little loco. 03013 looks like it has seen better days as it awaits its next shunting duty at York. The nearby BREL Works, carriage sidings, civil engineers/permanent way department, parcels vans and Motorail bay all provide it with work. This sunny-looking photograph was taken during July 1975, one year before it was withdrawn – unlike other 03s it didn't make it into preservation, and it was scrapped at Doncaster at the end of March 1977. I had taken a day trip to York whilst on a family holiday in Scarborough, where there was at least two 03s (complete with match trucks) out stationed for carriage shunting duties. Ever since I made a total mess of putting together an Airfix kit of the Drewry-built version of this narrow chimney 03, I have had a soft spot for them. I was six years old and got polystyrene glue everywhere it shouldn't be – perhaps that's why I photographed 03013 all those years ago?

Within sight of York Minster. The Minster is still there, but sadly such a fine line-up of ready-for-duty First Generation diesels is history. They are standing in the sidings close to York Depot during August 1975. I am glad I took lots of railway pictures whilst on day trips to York, rather than its ancient buildings. Unlike the ever-changing railway scene, they will still be there for generations to come.

Leeds Holbeck's Skin Head 31111 heads the far-left line of mixed traffic locos. Behind it is Healey Mills 40073, followed by a pair of 37s. 31111 was scrapped at BREL Swindon in July 1986. However, like a number of other no-longer-with-us locos I photographed, it has been modelled, in this case by Hornby in 00 gauge. The middle line-up is headed by a Class 46, followed by a pair of 37s. The 46 could have been a Gateshead- or Laira-allocated example, both found their way to York on Cross-Country passenger trains. The right-hand line also has two 37s in it, headed by Tinsley's 37121 waiting their next move – probably a South-Yorkshire-bound freight.

Carstairs Yard. Until electrification of the south-facing Carstairs triangle spur off the West Coast Mainline leading to Edinburgh, plenty of diesels were needed to be on-hand at this yard adjacent to the station. The electrification was completed during 1989, until then they'd be used to haul trains to and from Edinburgh. For many years electric-hauled trains ran into the station area, north of the triangle, where a diesel was coupled up to the rear to take the train on to Scotland's capital city. Such moves, of course, got more involved with Glasgow/Edinburgh trains that split and joined at Carstairs. In this case the electric loco would continue forward with the Glasgow portion. In the reverse, the diesel off the Edinburgh portion would come off at Carstairs and head to the yard in readiness for the next move. Nowadays this only happens at night when the multi-part Caledonian Sleeper splits/joins there. In this winter 1980 photo, Stratford-allocated Silver Roof 47521, Haymarket's 47517 and Eastfield's 27022 await their next duties. The 27 would have been used on freight, permanent way and parcels workings, the 47/5s on Inter-City passenger haulage.

3 PLACES TO GO & THINGS TO DO

From an early age, I recognised that railways are full of all sorts of people doing all sorts of things, going to all sorts of places – without them there would be no railway and no need for one. Its depots, stations, trains and yards are full of life, of onlookers, passengers, workers and visitors. The old saying *places to go and things to do* really does apply to the railway environment. It didn't take long before my curiosity engine kicked into gear asking myself the usual (and more unusual) people-watching questions. The endless list started to unfold. Dependent on the person and situation, the questions on the list included:

Where are they going?
What are they doing, and how long have they been doing it?
Where do they work, or which school do they go to?
Are they meeting someone?
Are they saying goodbye to someone?
How old are they?
Is the person married, or do they have a boyfriend or a girlfriend?
Do they like what they are doing?
Are they happy or unhappy?
Will they be going away for long?
Do they like train travel?
Do they like trains?
What did they have for breakfast?
Are they wearing their best clothes?
Are they well off or not?

The only problem was that I always ended up with lots of unanswered questions, and only expressions on their faces or body language gave any clue towards answering some of them – although I probably got it totally wrong. Regardless of the questions, people and other forms of life (animals and birds for example) are all part of the experience of going by train or visiting somewhere on the railway. They are noticed by some, but ignored intentionally or unintentionally by others.

Once I got to grips with my first proper camera in 1972, it soon dawned on me that, if I was to photograph as much of the British Rail scene as possible, living things would need to be included in my quest. In my mind, I had changed the other part of the old saying 'people to see', to 'people to photograph'. By this time, I had already looked at lots of my railway photographer heroes' (Colin T. Gifford and Eric Treacy) images, as well as the work of world-famous cameraman Cartier Bresson. They had all made a plain photograph into a winner by including people in it. They cleverly positioned people as the focal point or to one side of the composition, either in groups, randomly located or a solitary person. They were never posed, or at least not obviously. They taught me to cut across the old adage that people get in the way when photographing something, in my case British Rail. I reckoned, apart from adding human interest, this would add to the validity of what I was trying to do. We live in an ever-changing world, and our social history is being made every day, working practices are gradually changing. My thinking told me that, by including railway life in some of my photographs, one day they would provide an interesting insight into how things were or, in some cases, how they haven't changed at all. Whatever the result, I knew I would never be as good as my heroes, but I wanted to give it a go.

Partly for convenience, but mainly because funds were low, I used only a standard 50mm lens to take the photographs in this section. To avoid posed photographs, I casually included people in the shots – I reckoned that's how my hero photographers had achieved their master works. The approach did seem to work. I ended up with hundreds of photographs, a selection of which are included in this chapter. A few even include fellow rail enthusiasts, and I like to think they are still just as passionate or even more so about railways as I am.

If I have successfully put this chapter's photographs and words together, you will say that I managed to achieve what I had set out to do. Even better if they induce a few of those unanswerable people-watching questions and generate a few smiles. I have my fingers crossed.

West Country holiday train. London-Paddington-bound 1059 *Western Empire* arrives at Torquay with a morning train from Paignton, during July 1973. The assembled passengers would have been on a BR 'Golden Rail' package holiday, returning home after a holiday on the English Riviera. You can tell this because they are standing in the designated area for them. The reserved coach allocated to them would come to a stand alongside, almost like a military operation. Their package holiday would have included reserved seat train travel and a hotel – something that all the commercially savvy pre-Nationalisation railway companies introduced, to help ensure holidaymakers used 'their' seaside destinations' trains, hotels and ships. BR followed through with this initiative when they took over, later marketing it as 'Golden Rail', covering many popular starting points and destinations, including some served by its Sea Link shipping services. Just a thought – ten years earlier, the train in this photograph could have been hauled by a Castle or King Class steam loco and three years later a Class 50. This shows how short-lived the reign of the Class 52 Western was.

Paddington. The people in this shot are clearly in a rush and focused on where they are heading for. They have just arrived at London Paddington during the summer of 1980. After a long journey from the West Country or South Wales, they would have been keen to get the next stage of their journey underway. An FX4 taxi, Routemaster bus, the Underground or a walk would have come next. One of my favourite bits in this photo is the oil barrel, although 50035 *Ark Royal*, the HST and 50014 *Warspite* are pretty good too. Unlike 50014, which was scrapped in 1989, 50035 made it into preservation.

Opposite: **Time to open the flask and sandwiches.** It's early afternoon on 20 August 1980 at Peterborough. Definitely time to open the flask and sandwiches – probably better, and certainly a lot cheaper, than partaking in the station's Travellers Fare Buffet! I tended to do both, travelling around made me hungry and thirsty.

Here, 55004 *Queens Own Highlander* is arriving with 1D02, 12.05 Kings Cross–Hull, but the seated passengers clearly don't want to catch this train. They are probably waiting for one of the many other East Coast Mainline trains, quite a few still hauled by the mighty Class 55. Alternatively, they might have been waiting for the Class 31

hauled Birmingham–Norwich service. Whatever the case, they seem quite happy sat in the sun. Surprisingly, not one of them is looking at the spectacle of a Class 55 hauled Inter-City train, or me. 55004 looks in fine fettle, unlike twelve months earlier, when the loco had been languishing at BREL Doncaster waiting for power units. It arrived there on 28 April 1978 and didn't get released back into traffic until December 1979, a shortage of parts and industrial action having exacerbated the situation. This loco was not the only one to be affected, during October 1979 twelve other class members were undergoing or awaiting major remedial work at Doncaster.

School holidays. It's 20 August 1980, mid-way through the long school holidays, and these young chaps have got it made. What a fantastic way to while away the days at Peterborough, watching the vast array of trains approaching, departing and passing through the busy station. It's far better than going to school or work. One of them has made good use of the lamp post to prop up his racing bike; his day out would have been cheap, with no bus or train tickets to pay for. They are watching the departure of Finsbury Park allocated 55015 *Tulyar* hauling 1L43, 14.05 Kings Cross–York. It looks fantastic emblazoned with the depot's signature white cab livery. This loco was one of the last Deltics in service on BR, it lasted until 2 January 1982 before being sold to an enthusiast. It is now owned by The Deltic Preservation Society Limited.

Andrex or Izal? The question refers to the football fan leaning out of the carriage droplight with what looks like a toilet roll in his hand. I might be wrong though, it could be a bandage, bag or parcel.

This photo was taken in May 1977 towards the end of the football season. Gateshead-allocated 46039 is hauling a football train (Footex) out of Birmingham New Street. Back then, one of the less-menacing rituals of some football fans who travelled on them was making toilet paper rolls unravel whilst hanging out of the window. The resultant streamer would often be unfurled whist passing through stations. The answer to the heading's question is probably Izal; whilst shorter than Andrex, its more robust composition would have fared better especially at speed. Their more menacing activities were violence, loud chanting and train wrecking. Police horses and plenty of officers on foot were used to keep football train passengers together when they left and arrived at major railway stations. It was quite unnerving for other rail passengers, including me. I was surprised that BR tolerated it for so long.

Where are you going to? These two dogs look like they are talking to each other; perhaps they are asking each other where they are heading. The young sheepdog looks like it would really like to be off its lead and running about. A busy railway station full of people is not really the same as a big field with sheep in it, so it's perhaps just as well that it's on a lead. Meanwhile, the other dog looks at ease with its surroundings, probably a regular rail traveller. Perhaps he is reassuring the sheepdog that rail travel is rather good? Check out the very 1970s trousers of the passenger leaving the brake/guards section on the DMU! This shot was taken at Crewe during the summer of 1975.

Heading home from Skeggy. This busy scene, taken at Skegness during August 1980, was typical of each day at the seaside station. On my first visit, I was amazed how many trains served Skegness and how well-filled they were. Many of them were loco-hauled, making them a honeypot for rail enthusiasts. The station's concourse looks like it has changed little since steam days. The older waiting passengers have probably been holidaying there since they were the age of the youngsters in the photo. I wonder if any of the passengers had taken the bus from Butlins Holiday Camp.

Driver change. 81012, recently renumbered from E3014, receives a new driver for the next stage in its northbound Anglo-Scottish turn. The location is Crewe during the autumn of 1974, not long after the West Coast Mainline route to Glasgow was fully electrified. A year earlier, a diesel loco, probably a Class 40, 47 or 50, would have taken over this working at Crewe. Check out the driver's very 1970s sideburns. His bag looks well-filled and heavy; I guess he still has a long day ahead of him. There might well be a flask and sandwiches tucked away inside it for sustenance later in the day. The weight is clearly making it more difficult to climb into the cab.

Holiday perms. It's a sunny Saturday afternoon in August 1979 at Doncaster, perfect weather to start a holiday. The ladies sat at the compartment window seats on this Cleethorpes-bound Class 37 hauled train look a bit cluttered up with bags that probably contain something to eat on the journey. The ladies clearly wanted to look their best for the train ride and their holiday; it looks like they have recently had their hair permed, probably earlier in the day, their hair does look perfect. One has got a cardigan on, it's probably her favourite. The other has a Danimac-style coat on – it's probably her best. I hope they had a good holiday. The chap window hanging looks like he is poised ready for a fume-filled, but exhilarating, run to the coast.

Shoulders back. This station worker is clearly an ex-military man, wartime or National Service if he is younger than I am thinking. He clearly prides himself on his parade ground walk, no doubt instilled in him by a discipline-inducing sergeant. When I took this photo, on a May weekday during 1979 at Oxford, it was only thirty-four years since the end of the war, so BR and other employers throughout the land still had thousands, maybe millions, of wartime veterans on their books. The pairing of Class 37s (now-preserved 37206 is nearest) are hauling an empty train of quite new Amey Roadstone hopper wagons.

Waiting patiently. I used to regularly get taken to watch trains in my trolley, at my request. I can remember it vividly, despite only being little. It cemented my lifelong passion for railways; thank you, mum and dad. These chaps, including the trolley-bound infant, are patiently waiting for a steam loco to pass Edge Hill on 27 July 1980. It will be 5690 *Leander,* being used to haul special trains between Manchester Victoria and Liverpool Lime Street. Whilst waiting for 5690, they will have seen plenty of passing trains and no doubt looked across to the sidings full of ferry wagons. The trolley looks like a Mothercare model, quite a rarity nowadays. Its well-behaved passenger will be all grown up now, maybe a parent themselves. I wonder if each generation likes trains as much as the four men in the photo.

Hurry up! There's a feeling of urgency in this scene at Edge Hill one summer Saturday during 1980. The chap has clearly got off in a rush and the little girls' mum is smartly ushering them onto the train. I am wondering if the train is running late, maybe it left Lime Street late or it was held up at signals after leaving? Class 108, number M51912, is forming the 17.38 so stopping train service to Manchester Victoria.

Stop look and listen. These seated Army Cadets are doing exactly what it says on the sign; they have stopped whatever they were doing to look and listen. I am not sure what has caught their attention. They have been drafted in to help marshal the crowds that will be watching the Rocket 150 Rainhill Cavalcade pass later in the day. The cavalcade was comprised of locos and trains spanning from the earliest days of railways through to the latest, including one of the far from successful APTs. A temporary enclosure adjacent to the historic Liverpool– Manchester line, complete with grandstand seating, was built to enable the public to safely watch the spectacle. I paid £10 for a seat, programme and a DMU shuttle ride from Manchester Victoria to the event. Of course, many people didn't do things properly, unlike me, and chose to create their own viewing areas, standing by the lineside and on bridges to watch instead. Far cheaper, but they didn't get a ride on a specially drafted-in London-Marylebone-based DMU to/ from Manchester like I did.

Lovers Lane. What more could a loving couple want than a picturesque view of the eastbound Harwich Boat Train passing through Reddish Vale? Not only that, they have the comfort of a once plentiful, but now rare, Austin Allegro to sit in. Just in case they were on a secret liaison I made sure not to include the number plate when taking the photo. The train is being hauled by a Stratford-based Class 47, during the summer of 1974. The Buffet car was usually a pre-war Gresley, one of the last wooden-bodied coaches still in use on BR. Sadly, its Art Deco features had been stripped out and replaced with Mark 1 coach Formica finishes. To me, a teenager from Manchester with a few pence spending money to my name, the Harwich Boat Train sounded very special and unattainable. It was often filled with passengers travelling to or from the Continent – not as exotic and sophisticated as the *Orient Express*, but almost. Best of all it brought Eastern Region motive power to Manchester.

Angie. During the 1970s and 1980s, most depots and many stations had a cat. There are probably quite a few that still do. This is Angie, the Reddish depot cat. She looks clean, well-fed and contented. It could be because of her good job catching and eating plenty of mice, but it's more likely lots of food and milk given to her by the depot workers is the cause. Like all cats, she likes being off the ground – in her case, the Depot Foreman's hatch was a favourite place to while away the hours in comfort. I didn't know the cat's name until somebody wrote about her in an Amazon review for one of my previous books. I wonder if she was named after the brilliant Rolling Stones song?

Heading home. After an afternoon in town, passengers leave the trusty 504 set behind, which has just arrived from Manchester Victoria on a Saturday afternoon in May 1978. They all look like they are keen to get home: they have purpose in their stride. The guard is leaping aboard after dropping some paperwork off at the booking office. Any minute now, the train will depart for all stations to Bury Bolton Street.

What time is our train? This group of ladies, with the assistance of a member of the station staff, are looking at the large timetable poster on Manchester Victoria's Platform 12. They are all togged out for a day out; the lady in the foreground is wearing a smart handbag, dress suit and shoes specially for the July 1977 outing. They may well have been going to Blackpool – three car Class 104s arrived/departed from Platform 12, shuttling back and forth from Blackpool North filled with commuters, day trippers and holidaymakers. A fleet of thirteen were allocated to Newton Heath especially for use on this service. You could tell them apart from other Class members because they had a distinctive bold white stripe running along the bodyside, beneath the windows.

At one with the world. Beyond the smartly attired BR employee on Nottingham's Platform 4, you can see a chap heading towards us. He is also smartly togged out. From what I can see, he's looking very happy – totally at one with the world. Is it the thought of climbing aboard the Class 45 Hauled London Paddington-bound Inter-City service or something else that has put a smile on his face?

Bye bye. An afternoon service from Liverpool Lime Street to Newcastle is about to depart from Manchester Victoria during Easter 1978. This chap is waving goodbye to a group of ladies comfortably sat in a no-smoking designated part of a Mark 2 non-air-conditioned coach. It now seems hard to believe that people could smoke on trains; I did, until I gave up smoking in 1983. I reckon the ladies are on a day trip to York and the chap has given them a lift to the station. He would have had to buy a platform ticket to see them off as the ticket barrier staff were quite strict at Manchester Victoria.

Skeggy here we come! This driver is making his way to the leading Class 20 of this double-headed train to Skegness. His body language says to me he is not at all thrilled with the prospect of going to the seaside destination. He's probably driven trains, diesel and steam hauled, to the East Coast resort hundreds of times and was probably a bit weary of it all by then. At the time (August 1980), the Class 20 double-headed passenger trains that plied between the East Midlands and Skegness were well-loaded with excited day-trippers and holidaymakers, plus, of course, highly enthusiastic 20 bashers whose demeanours were in stark contrast to this chap's. I took this photograph at a gloomy looking Nottingham. You can tell that it's summer, though, by the reflection of the holiday-clothes-clad railway photographer in the Mark 1 window reflection.

Wash and brush up. This shot was taken at the doorway of Manchester Victoria's superb Edwardian washroom, during a summer morning in 1980. All the fittings were just as they were when installed by the Lancashire and Yorkshire Railway in 1909, and included vast sinks, shiny copper pipes, hot/cold taps, large mirrors, finished off with Art Nouveau and Harlequin style tiling. A delight to behold. Although, when I took the photo, they were understandably a little worn after over seventy years of use.

The chap, like thousands before him, is making full use of the free of charge facilities to freshen up and have a shave before the start of the day. The washroom decor and fittings were a million miles apart when compared with BR's new 'Supaloos' that were being opened at several major stations such as London Euston and Edinburgh. For me, and probably the man in the photo, Manchester Victoria's vintage version was far more appealing.

Let me carry your case. This Class 108 has just brought the lady with the case from Lancaster to Arnside on an April afternoon during 1973. It's likely she has travelled much further to visit her friend, who is keen to carry the suitcase. Are they relations, old friends from maybe school days or wartime? Has the lady who is meeting her friend lived there all her life or retired there? Lots of questions and no answers. I am sure I could come up with plenty more questions, that's the problem with people-watching. Check out the London Midland Region maroon enamel station sign, I bet someone now has it in their 'railwayana' collection.

I can reach! Determination prevails as this Western fan tries so hard to reach up to *Western Fusillier*'s cast D1023 number plate to undertake a brass rubbing of it, something lots of enthusiasts did back then. He had a far easier task than tracing the loco's nameplate in the same way, but a tall order nonetheless. Maybe he went on to doing that as well? A number plate and nameplate set would be the ultimate, collectors of the real thing are sure to agree. I didn't hang around to see how successful he was. Hopefully, he was pleased with the finished product; it might well be tucked away somewhere as a reminder of the day, 20 November 1976, a Western-hauled train came to York. D1023 brought the packed Western Talisman charter from and then back to London Kings Cross. The photo was taken in the yard that now forms part of the National Railway Museum.

Going to see a Deltic. This young enthusiast has a good mum, or it might be his equally good nana. Whoever it is, she is quite happily walking along York's Platform 16 during the winter of 1980. They are on their way to watch a Class 55 Deltic uncoupling from a Kings Cross–York service. I wonder if they had gone on an afternoon outing to the station specially to watch and spot trains. Alternatively, they might have been on their way home and he'd asked if they could see the loco up close. I think there is good chance the young lad, who'd be a bit older now, would instantly remember if he saw this photo.

Last-minute rush. In sharp contrast to the very sleepy, laid-back, platform scene at Kyle of Lochalsh three backpacker lads rush across the station yard to catch the train. They have just have just got off the Skye Ferry (now replaced by a bridge), but they can't have been on holiday for long, as the more relaxed West Coast of Scotland way of life hasn't yet rubbed off on them. The Class 26 hauled train will soon depart for Inverness, if it wasn't for the three lads nobody would ever guess. The photograph was taken in August 1979. The whole scene is packed full of yesteryear gems, it's one of my favourites for seeing how many I can find.

4 A DIFFERENT PERSPECTIVE

During the late 1960s and early 1970s, I used to sometimes go shopping in Stockport with my dad. One of our ports of call was WHSmith for a newspaper and a browse. It was a great place to visit because he loved books and I liked to dip into the railway magazines. If my spending money ran to it I'd even buy one. My favourite was the gen- and photo-filled *The Railway Magazine*. I even remember dad got a driver of the 11 Guinea end of BR steam excursion to sign the cover of my August 1968 issue! In September 1970, I moved to secondary school. Luckily, it had a well-stocked library and amongst its magazine rack was *The Railway Magazine*, which the school had a rolling subscription for, so there was no longer any need to buy it. I could spend hours in the library reading and looking at everything on its pages free of charge. Whilst doing so I was learning a great deal about railways, current and past. There was another magazine that I liked – *Railway World*. This was a little bit different, with glossy pages that brought out every detail of the high-quality photographs that appeared in it, and its photo-feature pages really did catch my eye. It was great for comparing photo styles. From time to time I'd spot an issue containing photographs that were different from the norm. It was a very avant-garde style known as the New Approach, which cut across long-held railway photograph taking convention. Colin T. Gifford, along with several others such as Ian Krause and the MNA (Masters Neverers Association), were pioneers. I was captivated by the way they turned their backs on taking perfectly-lit-from-behind three-quarter shots of trains – literally in some cases. The result had me captivated by their mix of arty and naturalistic styles. Trains were often apparently incidental, being just about or not even seen in their photographs. Cleverly, the trains were somehow seen clearly in the mind's eye, despite not being the focal point. The unorthodox compositions that often majored on people, infrastructure and general environment worked wonders.

In addition to those brilliant photographers' work, I was also wowed by a northern artist, Trevor Grimshaw. I first came across his moody industrial scenes in the Colin Jellicoe's art gallery on Portland Street in Manchester. He was going around the north-west capturing the final throws of the steam age and Industrial Revolution factories on canvas. The scenes he was portraying were all too familiar to me. Like the New Approach photographers, he was using his skills to capture the reality, rather than well-lit perfection. In later years, I used to see Trevor almost daily, as he lived just around the corner from work, but I was too in awe of him to talk to him and say how much I admired his work. Sadly, he died quite young in a house fire. If he was still alive now I would certainly make my admiration known to him. I have since talked to his friends about him, but it's not as good as talking to the man himself – if only I'd not been struck down with a reoccurring bout of shyness when I was a young chap!

What these people were doing was looking at and recording things with a different perspective. I believe it wasn't different at all. It was presenting the scene in a manner that reflects how and what we all look at every day. A perfectly tidy, well-composed and lit three-quarter image of anything isn't what we normally see. We are always looking at all sorts of things from odd angles in a wide range of situations, environments and light levels. Every day is filled with different perspectives, and we all individually perceive what we see. I reckoned that, to do my photographic mission justice, I had to try to adopt a similar approach to those people I have mentioned when taking some of my 1970s and '80s British Rail Scene shots. I ended up with quite a few: some worked well, some not. They might be liked by some people, but not others. I have picked out a few for this chapter. What do you think of them?

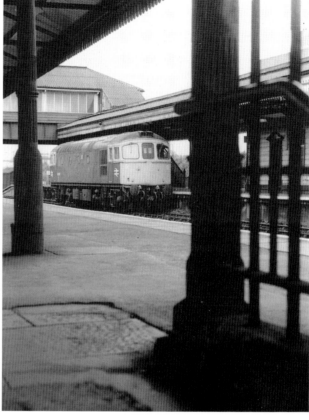

Waterloo stations. Viewed from between London Waterloo's stark, but immensely strong, station roof-supports, the 1946-built Class 405 (4SUB), number 4127, EMU arrives as empty stock. This move was in preparation for the imminent rush hour, in a matter of minutes after this photo was taken it would start to fill with homeward-bound commuters. This is one of those views we all have had while walking towards the end of a platform to watch the comings and goings of a busy railway station, but perhaps it hasn't been photographed? The buffet car train is soon to depart with a service to Exeter St Davids, via Salisbury, hauled by a Western Region (ex-London Midland Region) Class 50. Being a chap from the north-west who well remembers Class 50s in and around Manchester, it looked out of place in such a deeply Southern Region railway environment. The photograph was taken in the second week of August 1981.

At the top of the steps. How many of us have climbed or run up railway station steps to reach platform level, keen to see what there is to see? Invariably climbing them two at a time and not holding the handrail, in a mad rush, more often than not after a hell-for-leather run down steps leading from the opposite platform. Something I still do from time to time, despite my advancing years. This shot was taken just after I'd reached the top of a flight of stairs at Clapham Junction. I can remember being a bit weary at the time after a mega station bash in the capital. On this occasion, I definitely used the handrail to help haul myself up the stairs, it's visible to the right of the photograph. My efforts were rewarded with the sight of 33006 heading out of London; it tells me that I don't always have to rush up steps to bag a 'just in time' shot of a loco or train. I took this photograph during Easter 1980.

The football pitch. I took this dramatic photo of a not-very-dramatic scene at Thirsk one Saturday afternoon in September 1980. I stumbled on the desolate place outside Thirsk station – I can only guess the football team was playing away that day. I was making my way to the East Coast Mainline racing stretch, south of the town, on a mission to photograph Class 55 Deltics at speed. My efforts ultimately proved to be very worthwhile, however, I much prefer this shot. The football club had made good use of the ancient pre-Grouping railway carriage, reminiscent of the one seen in the *Titfield Thunderbolt* film. I reckon it wouldn't have lasted much longer, it looked rather worse for wear after nearly a century of use. Did it survive?

Tyneside Deltic. Not a bridge, castle, large track complex or vast station to be seen – all of which often feature in railway photographs taken at Newcastle. Instead, I plumped for this shot, taken against a threatening sky whilst on a brief visit there during 1977. Only having a few minutes before I departed south, hauled by this Class 55, I fancied composing a shot attempting to demonstrate the loco's superior power and ability. Did my attempt work? I would have liked to take some photographs of the train in the station too, but there wasn't enough time. I did go back to Newcastle whilst 55s were still in service, to take more traditional photographs but, sadly, I couldn't afford to have the films developed. Worse still, I lost them at some time in the distant past.

Sparrow talk. While wandering around York station awaiting the next Class 55 hauled service from London Kings Cross, for some reason I looked up and saw these two sparrows. They looked as if they were talking to each other. Being late October 1980, most trees had lost their leaves, so I guess a signal ladder was as good as, if not better than, a bare tree branch – especially as it provided a high and solid perch alongside a railway station full of things to eat. Having my camera to hand in readiness for the sound of Napier engines approaching, I was able quickly bag this photo. The signals were in the yard adjacent to Platform 16.

Tail lamp at the ready. Scarborough in the 1970s and 1980s was a surprisingly good location to photograph loco-hauled trains. The degree of activity generated by excursions and service trains was brilliant, probably better than other enthusiast seaside terminus honeypots such as Blackpool, Great Yarmouth, Llandudno and Skegness. Class 25, 31, 37, 40, 45, 46, 47 and even 55 locos were a regular feature, while Mark 1 and 2 coaches were shunted to allow incoming locos to be released from the station's cul-de-sac platforms. This was undertaken by a couple of 03 shunters outstationed from York Depot. It was always handy to have a tail lamp located in strategic places in readiness to be placed at the end of a string of westbound coaches – this one has probably been removed from the first-class coach alongside it.

Buffer stop. On 20 November 1976, York yard was filled with enthusiasts wanting to admire, cab and photograph 1023 *Western Fusilier*, which had just arrived hauling the Western Talisman excursion from London Kings Cross. The crowds made it difficult to get many decent shots, so I decided to take a different photographic tack. I wandered up the yard and left the crowds behind, and I ended up with this slightly off-beat shot, where people are still in the photo but don't drown the loco. I do like to have people in photographs, but not overwhelming the composition. I think it works. In addition, I was able to include the buffer stop as well as some less-photographed items of railway interest, such as the ex-LMS coach, standing alongside, that was used as an observation car/saloon for BR directors and managers. Several of which were still in use and some eventually made it into preservation.

Wrong line working. This was a different perspective for me, but one that many foreigners have of their own railway systems, as their trains always run on the right. I took this photograph just before the Class 47 hauled Harwich Boat Train plunged into the 3-mile 950-yard Totley Tunnel at Grindleford one Saturday in the summer of 1978. Necessary engineering work was required inside the tunnel which required one line to be closed to trains – you can see the red flag between the rails protecting the closed section of line. Not a foolproof approach to health and safety, especially in the dark! Nowadays, I guess both lines would be closed and a bus service provided to get people to Sheffield, or train services would be rerouted. At the time, the train could have been routed via Woodhead. I would have much preferred this option, especially as I never did get to ride on a train over the electrified Trans-Pennine line.

Against the light. In the 1970s, I occasionally read *Amateur Photography* magazine, which was packed full of adverts, articles, competitions, photo features and reviews. One of the first things I read was a feature on '*contre jour*' photographs, which turned out to be fancy way of describing photos taken against the light or into the sun. Until then, it was something I steered away from. I still had in my mind the well-known basic of ideally having the sun behind me when taking a photograph. The feature quickly taught me otherwise. By taking into the sun, I could bag some vivid light and dark shots of the BR network, often bringing out certain features that would otherwise be lost in a conventional photograph.

The lack of masses of detail makes this image hard to date. It could have been taken in 1950s. It was, in fact, taken on 19 April 1980 at Manchester Victoria. The Black Five steam loco is 5000, it double-headed with 80079 hauling The Black Countryman railtour from Hereford via Chester, Skelton Junction, Guide Bridge and Miles Platting. My photographic approach has accentuated the loco's distinctive profile and steam but more importantly for me are the cast iron bridge parapets, diamond crossing and towering lamp post. You wouldn't get me climbing up the ladder to change the light bulb, not even for a million pounds. I don't like heights and value my life. I wonder if anyone still changed the light bulb or if it was redundant – if they did, I hope it was a long-lasting, heavy-duty type that didn't need regular replacement. The scene looking in this direction out of the station is now very much changed, the lamp post has been felled and the diamond crossing removed.

Now you see it, now you don't. For just a few seconds there's a Class 76 clearly visible through the shrubbery. I must admit, I grabbed this photo at a moment's notice. I could hear the rumbling of a loco as I tried to find a good lineside location at Hadfield. It was early evening after work, June 1980 and I had just parked my VW Beetle up. By this time, the Woodhead route and its Class 76s life was nearly at an end, so every photo was important – I just had to secure this one of 76006 heading light engine to Guide Bridge Stabling Point. This loco lasted right to the end, surviving until 20 July 1981, and it was scrapped at Rotherham in May 1983. This shot reminds me of the many times I have walked on a path or driven on a road alongside a vegetation-lined railway only able to get an intermittent view of it, a 'now you see it, now you don't' view of any passing trains.

Sterilised and pasteurised. Food and drink is an important element in running a railway. This is confirmed with this photograph of empty milk bottles and a mixing jar on a window ledge in Reddish Depot's canteen, in February 1979. The bottle on the left used to hold the oddly tasting sterilised milk, often known as 'Stera', now a very rare commodity but once common and preferred by many, but not me. The other two milk bottles once contained pasteurised milk. I don't like the look of the translucent jar – even from the outside its contents appears to have seen better days. The canteen had a great view of locos lined up ready and waiting for their next duties, as demonstrated by 76010, whose pantographs are raised, drawing power from the dc overhead catenary.

Lost link. I wonder how many bits and pieces, large or small, that BR lost over the years. Did this coupling get reused or lie forlorn between the rails at Reddish Depot for years? I reckon there's a good chance the latter occurred and it was scrapped when the sidings were ripped up, after the depot closed. The EMU trailer car in the centre background belongs to a Class 304; it had been brought to Reddish for wheelset attention. The loco visible to the left of the photograph is pioneer Class 24, number 24005 (D5000), waiting to be towed away for scrapping. To the far right are Class 506s, waiting for the start of the following day's rush hour. This photograph was taken one Sunday afternoon in October 1975.

Wagon wheels. Don't be alarmed, I hadn't risked life and limb to take this unusual photograph. It was taken underneath a mile-long string of vintage wagons that had not moved for a long time. They were waiting for scrapping, a bit like being on Death Row I guess. At the time, there wasn't just one line, there were two! It wasn't just Woodhams at Barry that had a glut of things to scrap, there were a large variety of types including bitumen, coal, coke and tank wagons. Many were of riveted construction, and some had seen use before Grouping in 1923. Not only were they veterans of the BR Network, but some had come out on NCB and ICI industrial railway systems.

Where was this phenomenal sight you may ask? It was between Denton and Reddish South on the once four-track route, which is now largely singled.

Two of the running lines had become redundant and used for wagon storage by Standard Railway Wagon. They had workshops adjacent to Reddish South station, where they built, maintained and scrapped wagons. Over the years, the scrap line dwindled to 'hardly any' and none replaced them, the supply of redundant wagons having been exhausted. The workshops eventually closed and all work was transferred to the company's main factory at Green Lane in Heywood, which in turn closed during the early 1990s. The main workshops have been redeveloped as an industrial estate, but its yard is now the site of the ELR's Heywood railway station.

A full load of spoil. BR's Engineering Departments used a wide array of wagons, many very old. You could identify them by their type names stencilled on the side plates; curiously, they bore no relationship to the wagon's use, instead they were named after marine life. The wagons seen in this photograph are the relatively modern Grampus, which proved to be quite versatile. In this case they are being used to transfer spoil and spent ballast to a BR tip. The train is heading west through Manchester Victoria, hauled by a Class 25. On this sunny Sunday in August 1979, I managed to compose this unusual angle shot by leaning out of a droplight window on an adjacent passenger train. It was hauled by a Class 45 destined for Liverpool Lime Street.

Destined for preservation. During the Rainhill 150 celebrations in 1980, BR's erstwhile Liverpool Road Goods Depot was opened to exhibit preserved, waiting to be preserved and current traction/rolling stock. The goods depot and adjacent original Liverpool and Manchester station were soon afterwards restored and transformed into the ever-popular Manchester Museum of Science and Industry. Over the years it has got better and better, the working museum houses a myriad of vintage gems, not just those related to the locality's railway history.

24081 was withdrawn soon afterwards and then preserved at the short-lived Steamport railway centre in Southport. It was the last Class 24 to be withdrawn, but now hauls trains at the Gloucestershire Warwickshire Steam Railway. I took this photograph after climbing aboard a modern flatbed wagon coupled to the loco. At the time officials didn't bat an eye lid at my chosen vantage point – I am sure they would now! Climbing on wagons would be frowned upon in our health and safety conscious, claim-filled world.

Monkey bridge. When I was growing up, any bridge with intermediate arched spars linking a bridge's two parapets seemed to be called a 'monkey bridge'. You can easily guess why. Likewise, climbing frames at local parks were called monkey bars by their users, me included. In the case of railway monkey bridges, I sometimes saw youngsters using them to do some crazy things. In addition to swinging from spar to spar, they were used to aid access on and off high flat top parapets, and the totally reckless would even climb over the sides. All a bit scary for me. I guess they were circus trainees. I visited this footbridge many times, but never saw any acrobatics; the unusually high bars and parapets were probably a bit off-putting, or perhaps because there must have been at least twelve electrified running lines beneath it. The location is Guide Bridge on an autumn afternoon in 1979. My photo angle is meant to accentuate the height of the unusually high parapets and length of footway, as well as focus on the group of sensibly clad spotters grouped at the far end, where there was a great vantage point for all the location's many daily moves.

Wath puddle. On a quiet Saturday afternoon in 1980, shortly after an April shower, I took this photograph of 76046 on shed at Wath Depot. This reflection shot was meant to induce a melancholy feeling. It did all seem a bit sad whilst wandering round the silent depot, knowing that soon the Class 76s stabled there would be withdrawn, and the lines that they ran on would be closed or brutally rationalised. Not only that, there was a curious sense that the nearby collieries were on borrowed time, which eventually did prove to be the case. Puddles are here today and gone tomorrow, much like what you can see in them, and that certainly applies to this one. My effort worked for me, I must admit to feeling a little bit melancholy as I write this caption.

Ladies room. Sometimes when in search of something different to photograph, or an unusual camera angle to try, the subsequent result didn't turn out as well I hoped. I am not sure if this is a hit or a miss. What do you think of this multi-reflection shot? Can you make the loco out? It's a Class 40 awaiting its next duty, and it's possible to see its driver sat in the cab. Can you see the Ladies Room sign? Rooms just for ladies were becoming a rarity in the 1970s. Can you determine the location? Well its Manchester Victoria, I think Platform 12, but I'm not sure. I bet someone out there can instantly confirm or refute that. The detail on the back of the photographs tells me it was taken during April 1979.

My first attempt. This is the first 'different perspective' photograph I ever took. It's the type of view all rail passengers see – a platform sign, station paraphernalia and trains in the background. One of those views they see, but tend not to see, if you know what I mean. I like to think it works.

However, it now looks very vintage. It's such a long time since I took this photo at Stockport station in November 1972, there's so much of it that's now part of railway history. I can spy quite a few 'must-haves' for railwayana collectors and railway preservationists. To take this shot, I had to stand on a box on top of a post office trolley. I also had to stand at an odd angle to dodge some sticky out bits; all very precarious, but worth it. Check out the Buxton-allocated Class 104, complete with the depot's signature white cab roof that's arriving on the far side of the station.

Out of the dark came light. It's a Sunday afternoon in March 1974 at Manchester Victoria. After a long subterranean walk through the gloomy glazed-brick subway, these steep steps leading to Platform 14 and 15 greet the two chaps with light. It's one of those views that travellers are generally pleased and relieved to see, but is rarely photographed. The top of the steps is the next stage in a journey somewhere, one step nearer or further away. The chap on the right is on his way to work, he's the driver of the next train to Leeds via Todmorden. The other is about to board it. I know because I was travelling with him, he's one of my schoolmates.

A low perspective. I have endeavoured to highlight the sweeping entrance to Llandudno Junction carriage sidings with this low-level shot. I have also tried to bring out the picturesque location, and the towering steam-age yard lamps (electric and gas). The flowers are an important element as well although I don't know what they are called. Another gen gap filling job for readers of this book. In the left-hand distance 1950s and earlier buildings are all that remain of the once busy steam shed, demolished during the 1960s. I took this photograph whilst on a family holiday at Llandudno in May 1976.

Redundancy. During the 1970s, the last of BR station gas lamps were being quickly made redundant due to the introduction of starkly modern electric versions. By the time I first set out with my camera, the Victorian-designed gas lamps, with their distinctive warm glow, were on borrowed time. Soon I would no longer be able to gaze at a lamp's glowing gauze mantle and its naked pilot light encased in a glass bowl – almost as mesmerising as gazing into a coal fire. After they had been replaced by an electric lamp, it was common for their vandalised remains to linger on until the scrap man arrived. This is an example of a lamp at this sad stage in its life, standing sentinel over a rapidly changing railway scene. It was taken at Denton station in February 1974.

A little bit of settlement. I took this photograph because of the interesting mix of inclined angles of the walkway, walls, handrail, bollards and railway beyond. Hundreds of thousands of people must have walked along this route – I wondered how many had photographed the scene, especially on a cold, snowy day. It wasn't until many years later, when I scanned the contact print of this image, that the cracks in the wall were noticed; clearly there had been some crack-inducing settlement taking place. I guess it got repaired, eventually. If it happened nowadays, the route would probably have been closed on safety grounds. The location is Rock Ferry, during the winter of 1978. The Class 105 DMU disappearing into the distance is on a service from Chester.

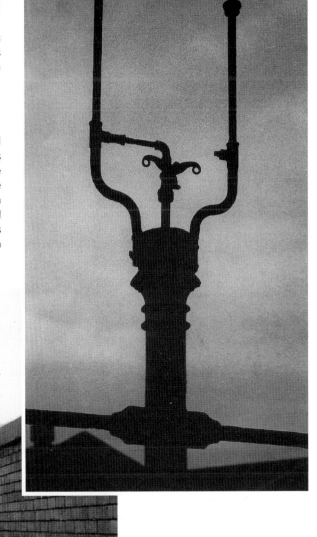

Poles apart. Railway lines used to be easier to pick out when viewed from a distance, thanks to the telegraph poles that skirted them for miles on end, but BR gradually felled them, putting the wires they carried into ducting alongside or beneath the running lines. Being out of harm's way, the amount of money and inconvenience saved on repairs must have been considerable. However, their rapid disappearance during the 1970s and 1980s meant that another reminder of the Britain's railway history would soon be all but extinct. Some still exist, but maybe only a few like the ones in this photograph. I wanted the passing train to be incidental, focussing attention on the poles, because the opposite approach usually prevailed. I took the photograph alongside the North Wales Mainline at Prestatyn during 1974.

50 arrival. I was walking along Paddington's platform to photograph this Class 253 Inter-City 125 HST, when I noticed the Class 50 hauled train arriving with a Torbay service. As it was a 50, I just had to press the shutter – they were too good to miss. It's another of those 'grab' shots which ended up reflecting how scenes are often seen but not photographed. My intention was to photograph the HST in the standard three-quarter manner, which I did afterwards but, of the two, I like this one far better. Not long after this, the 253 departed for Bristol Temple Meads. I took the photo one Saturday afternoon during July 1979.

5 INCLEMENT WEATHER

For me, biting cold winds, fog, mist, ice, rain and snow all fall into the inclement weather category. The type of weather that cancels long-awaited events and outings and has spoilt many a day out or holiday. How many of us have looked out on rain-soaked beaches with a miserable face? How many of us have said 'rain, rain, go away, come again another day' or 'it's raining, it's pouring, the old man is snoring'? Quite often inclement weather is not associated with taking photographs as the camera is left tucked away in the belief that it will be damaged and only poor photographs can be taken in challenging weather conditions. However, for me, bad weather is the best weather to take photographs. I hope when you cast your eye over the photographs in this chapter you don't think they would have looked better taken on a perfect sunny day.

Bad weather exudes atmosphere. Low light, overcast skies, reflections, accentuated light/dark details, shadows, rain soaked people and objects all combine to make a photograph that has atmosphere. Sunny day photographs don't have the same effect. British days are more prone to inclement weather, so a photograph taken in such conditions is something that perhaps better reflects reality – I felt that I needed to take lots of this type of photograph to accentuate and convey how Britain's railways looked during the 1970 and '80s. It also meant that my photographic activities weren't confined to barracks when the sun wasn't shining. A win–win for me.

Whilst my camera fared quite well in bad weather, quite often I didn't and neither did my clothes. Slips on ice on platforms and in railway yards were commonplace. Slithering down really yucky slag heaps when on location at coal mines are especially memorable! Frozen fingers, so cold that I couldn't properly press the camera shutter or wind on the film made these essential jobs a lot more awkward than on a warm day. Gloves were not an option, as I wouldn't have been able to handle my camera effectively with them on. Rain dripping down my face off my trusty bush hat wasn't good, and leaking shoes caused damp socks, which made me shivery. To help overcome the effects of the cold and damp I wore a parka coat or a big overcoat purchased at a bargain price from the Army and Navy Stores on London Road in Manchester (they also stocked vests and long johns, which helped me beat the elements). A steaming cup of Travellers Fare Bovril was also very welcome. Crewe station buffets excelled in making this dark, meaty tasting brew. I can smell and taste it right now.

Travelling light also helped, so my camera equipment was kept to a minimum, with just one camera fitted with a standard 50mm lens. A UV filter helped protect the lens when wiping off condensation. I remember a driver of one of the saddle tank steam locos at Agecroft Power Station using a dirty rag to clean the lens of my Pentax – thank goodness I had the filter on, imagine how I would have felt if I hadn't and the lens ended up badly scratched! I wouldn't have said anything to the driver, I wouldn't want to upset him. I always carried a couple of Ilford HP5 or Kodak Tri-X films (slower speed films were not up to the low light conditions) as I didn't want to ever be without film and sometimes I'd find myself miles away from a shop that stocked it. Tripods I owned, but never used as I found they got in the way. For slow shutter speed shots, I rested my camera on a solid surface, such as a platform edge, rail head, post office trolley or window ledge. Sometimes this resulted in odd reactions from onlookers. One time I remember lying on the platform face down at Sheffield taking a photo. Someone shouted, 'man down!' and then a small group of station workers came running towards me. I stood up and thanked them for their concern. I am not sure if they responded with a smile or a grimace.

I hope you enjoy this selection of inclement weather photographs and they encourage fellow photographers to take lots of pictures in theoretically poor conditions – but please don't be non-safety conscious like I was. I am more careful now!

Disappointingly wet. I took this photo in Torquay of a Class 47, number 1596, shortly after arriving on an October 1973 BR day excursion from Manchester Piccadilly. The loco had brought us from Birmingham New Street, where it had replaced a Class 85. Throughout the journey, it rained. I was with one of my mates and kept assuring him that the weather would be fantastic when we got to our destination. Just a few months previously I had been there on a two-week family holiday. The sun had shone every day, it was hot and the sky was blue – plus, there were lots of Westerns. I had it in my mind that this was always the case. How wrong I was. The rain was a real disappointment. We must have brought it with us from Manchester. Perhaps it was a rare occurrence, because the signalman is peering out of his signal box with a degree of curiosity. Having not seen any Westerns on our journey, I suggested that we go to Newton Abbot Depot in search of some. We had no problem getting in, but guess what? There were none there. Only two 47s and a Class 33. All in all, it was a bit of a wash out. A few months later, 1596 was renumbered 47470 and, in 1983, it was named *University of Edinburgh*. Sadly, it had a relatively short life for a 47, and it was scrapped in June 1995.

It's just stopped raining. A torrential April 1981 shower has just abated. After sheltering in cavernous London Waterloo for a while, I ventured out to the platform end in search of something to photograph. I wasn't disappointed on this occasion. I found the perfectly positioned 73110 carrying a 92 headcode, indicating that it was on a Waterloo to Weymouth semi-fast, via Eastleigh, on haulage duties. Further back, separated by a reflection-filled platform are 09005 and an unidentified Class 73. During my early days of spotting, pre-TOPS numbering, I didn't realise there was a variant of the Class 08 that would become the Class 09. A few years after that, I saw one for myself. They were quite a rarity.

Paddington reflection. Inter-City 125, 253006 heads out of Paddington into the damp London suburbs with a Bristol-bound service. Entering the station is a Class 117 DMU with a stopping train service from Reading. I was drenched taking photos at the unsheltered end of the station, but really enjoyed myself. I threw caution to the wind, ignoring the risk of catching my death of cold or double pneumonia – I was lucky I didn't succumb to either. I might now though, being much older. I particularly like the reflection of the signal gantry in this shot, which was taken during the winter of 1979.

Waiting. It's not long stopped raining: the wet rails, sleepers and platform bear vivid testament to the heavens having opened over Reading. This Class 47 is at the head of a London Paddington to Manchester Piccadilly service during July 1981. It is waiting to depart. The heavy cloud and dull weather suggest there is another downpour imminent. It's a waiting game – will it come before it departs or whilst underway, somewhere near Didcot maybe? In fact, we left the rain cloud behind.

I remember getting into conversation with a lady on the journey from Paddington. She asked me where I was going to and I said 'Manchester'. She was only going as far as Reading. She seemed surprised I wasn't taking the direct route from Euston: when I said, 'I want to take the long way around', she looked at me oddly. I guess she didn't relish circuitous train journeys like me. After we said our goodbyes, I took this photo from one of the train's Mark 2 coach droplights. I wonder if she got wet on her way home, or if she remembers me. The respective answers are probably 'yes' and 'no'.

Wet and gritty. Birmingham New Street was a cold, wet and a rather gritty looking place on the day I took this shot. It's November 1976, and Class 304, number 020, is waiting to depart with a service to Walsall. I can imagine its passengers were glad to climb aboard. The 304s typically had good heaters, well-sprung/stuffed seats and plenty of them, although window condensation could be a problem on days like this. This combined with cigarette smoke in coaches, where smoking was allowed, did have a negative effect on the 304's many positive attributes. The Class 45 is ready to depart with a West-Country-bound service. There won't be many holidaymakers on board. It will be a few months before this service is once again filled with passengers heading for the English Riviera.

Wellingtons needed. I could have done with a pair of wellingtons when I took this photograph at their namesake station in Shropshire. My well-worn suede Hush Puppies were not up to the job. I always bought Hush Puppies, my mates called them 'Joby Sneakers'. It had been raining for ages on this afternoon in spring 1976, as you can probably tell from the sopping wet platforms. The driver is peering out of his droplight to see if everyone is aboard, prior to getting the buzzer from the guard and then departing from Wellington. It looks like there is a bit of delay being caused by the brake/guard's section of the Class 101 DMU being loaded. The train is destined for the London Midland Region's Wolverhampton High Level on a service from Shrewsbury. At the time, the ex-GWR/Western Region Low Level station still existed, and it was used as a parcel depot. Until the late 1960s, Paddington, Shrewsbury and Birkenhead express passenger trains served the station. The last local trains from a decimated Birmingham Snow Hill ran until 1972. By then Snow Hill was like a ghost station, all its main line services had been diverted to New Street. By the summer of 1981, the parcel depot had closed, and the Low-Level station and its environs have since been redeveloped.

Soggy Shrewsbury. There's rain soaked atmosphere aplenty in this shot, taken at Shrewsbury during a spurt of station activity on a morning in March 1976. Cardiff-based Class 120 DMU set C611 has recently arrived with a Central Wales line service from Swansea. The car in the foreground, W50662, is fitted with a headlight to help the driver see more when nocturnally navigating the narrow, winding single-line route. The Class 116 Suburban DMU alongside will later form a service to Wolverhampton, and alongside it is a Class 101 that has just arrived from Chester. It will return soon afterwards.

Heading for Shrewsbury. My second favourite First Generation DMU is the Park Royal Class 103 (the Class 124 is my favourite). In this picture, an example leaves well-watered Machynlleth on an Aberystwyth to Shrewsbury service. The Class 116 in the siding, alongside the old loco depot that was by then a stabling point, had terminated at the Mid-Wales town. It's a Saturday in October 1976 and the winter timetable has started, if it had still been summer, Class 25 or 40 locomotives would have been hauling the 'Saturdays Only' holidaymaker trains. I remember, on that day, there was a Class 25 at the stabling point on hand for freight trip workings, train rescue and permanent way duties.

Grim Crewe. This photo was taken during December 1978. The weather was that bad I had to push the exposure on the Ilford HP5 film I was using in my Pentax camera, as 400 ASA wasn't fast enough. A darkening sky, thawing ice and a feeling of hanging damp made Crewe a grim place to be that day. I didn't mind, it was far more photogenic than on a perfectly sunny day. The steam is leaking nicely from beneath the Class 25 and the Western Region Mark 1 coach it is coupled to. The three window hangers aboard the Cardiff-bound train don't seem to mind the bitter cold; they look suitably clad for a thrash towards Shrewsbury and beyond. They must have been extremely keen 25 bashers. Arriving from the south is a Class 86/2 bound for Liverpool Lime Street.

Arrivals and departures. I am not alone as I bag this photo at Stoke-on-Trent on a very wet summer afternoon in 1979. There's another enthusiast present – you can see him towards the end of the platform I'm standing on. He must be as damp as me. The Class 120 DMU is arriving with a Crewe to Lincoln service, while the Class 304 is departing with an all stations to Manchester Piccadilly working. The 08 is shunting empty coal wagons that will soon be collected by a Class 25, which will take them for reloading at a Staffordshire colliery. At the time there were five: Hem Heath, Holditch, Silverdale, Victoria (Biddulph) and Woolstanton.

Arctic conditions. It was cold when I stood at the end of Rock Ferry station to photograph this Class 503 electric train departing for Birkenhead and Liverpool Central via the BR Mersey Tunnel. It was November 1978 and it well and truly felt like a winter's day. You might wonder why the buffer stops on the bay platforms in the foreground are the opposite way around to usual – they would normally look inwards towards a station, not outwards towards the outside world. After the closure of the ex-GWR Birkenhead Woodside terminus in 1967, Rock Ferry became the end of the line for remaining services from Chester and Ellesmere Port/Helsby. The buffer stops blocked off access to the old route beyond to Woodside. Until the extension of the Merseyrail electrified rail network to Chester and Ellesmere Port in 1985 DMUs worked these services. They would terminate in the bays, which enabled passengers to cross platforms to/from the electric trains serving Birkenhead and Liverpool. Rock Ferry therefore became a nicely laid out interchange station. Until 1967, when Woodside closed, loco-hauled passenger trains ran to/from London Paddington through Rock Ferry. At the time of my photograph, locos still passed through with freights serving the Birkenhead dock area, dead EMU haulage and light engine moves to/from Mollington Street Depot. I didn't wait around long enough to see any.

Next stop Liverpool James Street. Soon after taking the arctic photo at Rock Ferry, I took this one at Birkenhead Central. The appeal of a warm and cosy Class 503 had briefly got the better of me, and as a result I climbed aboard one at Rock Ferry. However, the sensibility of my quest to take all sorts of photographs depicting the BR scene quickly returned. After a short journey, I got off at Central, where trains enter and leave the tunnel that takes them under the River Mersey. I took this shot of leading Class 503, number M29279M, just before its subterranean run to Liverpool James Street. The chap standing alongside looks a bit cold. The reason for disembarking at Birkenhead Central station was to take photos at the adjacent EMU depot, which had an ample covering of snow.

Birds in flight. Is it the pressing of my clunky Russian Fed camera shutter or the driver bringing on the Class 100 DMU's power that has made these three pigeons take flight? On the other hand, they might be flying around just to keep warm. The DMU is bound for Buxton, filling in for a non-available White Cab Class 104. The driver is about to ease his train out of Stockport, but when he gets to the almost 1,000 feet above sea level destination the snow will be much deeper. Class 304 EMU, number 011, is between duties. The destination blind says Alderley Edge – I reckon that it will change to Crewe or Stoke-on-Trent, the usual southerly direction destination for 304s serving Stockport. Curiously, Stockport now has an extra platform known as Platform 0 where 011 is standing. I wonder how many other stations in the world have a Platform 0. Beyond is the goods yard, which included an NCB Coal Distribution Depot. Nowadays younger people would never believe it was ever there; as the yard has been totally redeveloped and looks very modern. Close to the entrance of the Coal Depot there is now a McDonald's.

White Christmas. I took this photo of a Class 37 hauled Blue Circle Cement train heading east, soon after it had left Earles Sidings during the week between Christmas and New Year 1976. I was on a hiking holiday with my mates, using youth hostels for overnight accommodation. At the time, there was a murderer on the loose, and whilst trudging along in the snow we entertained ourselves coming up with all sorts of scary scenarios. The two we ended up thinking most likely were that we'd encounter the murderer on the way to the next youth hostel or he'd break in and get us during the night. Believe it or not, to avoid the risk of the latter, we barricaded ourselves in the deserted youth hostel dormitory we stopped at that night. We wondered if other youth hostellers had cancelled their stay because of the weather or because the risk of being murdered in their cotton sleeping bag was too great. In hindsight, the hostel was probably empty because nobody else wanted to go on a Peak District hiking holiday during the Christmas festivities. Fortunately, the murderer was captured the following day and we completed our three-day adventure safely. Phew!

Royal Scot approaches. During late September 1973, a pair of Class 50s race through Warrington Bank Quay station with the London–Euston-bound Royal Scot. This was a truly impressive sight. I only just bagged this shot, I nearly missed taking it. I was sheltering from the torrential rain, with a couple of mates, under the station canopy. We were joking about something and briefly not taking notice of any train activity. Then one of them said that there was a train coming, I looked up, saw it was approaching at high speed and leapt into action. I only just managed to get into position and check my shutter speed. On this occasion, a high shutter speed was preferable to a clarity-enhancing small aperture. The train's next stop was Crewe, where the 50s were replaced by a Class 86 that would haul it south to Euston. One year later, the West Coast Mainline north of Crewe to Glasgow would become fully electrified and the days of 50s hauling Anglo-Scottish express trains would be at an end. On the left platform, you can see one of my mates imitating me leaping into action.

Green 40. On the same rainy day that I photographed the double-headed Class 50 Royal Scot thundering through Warrington Bank Quay, I took this shot of BR green-liveried Class 40, number 337 (40137). It's heading north with 6M86, the Severn Tunnel Junction to Carlisle freight. I can write this information with confidence because John Stephens, the Chairman of the Class 40 Preservation Society, told me so. He is an astonishing font of knowledge and has a brilliant memory, so thank you, John. The train was made up of mainly Vanfit wagons, and I can't help wondering what's inside them. The loco is still in its original BR green livery, updated with an all-over yellow front end. Originally the yellow would have only covered the lower section beneath the headcode boxes. The green livery, numbers and BR emblem are all rather faded – could it be that the substances that the loco had been washed in had not worked as they should? Not only did it remove the dirt, it removed the paint.

Winter in Hyde. I took this photograph during my dinner hour – I had just started working at the factory in the background. You can tell it was taken during the winter; the trees are bare, there's ice on the sleepers and the sky is heavy. It will certainly rain or go dark before morning. The year is 1975, the location is Hyde. The Class 105, on the left, is heading for Hyde Central station en route to Manchester Piccadilly. The Class 100 is making its way towards its next stop at Woodley, en route to Marple Rose Hill, and it will soon cross Apethorne Junction, which linked to the Woodhead route at Godley Junction. At the time, the junction was very busy with freight train movements, particularly Merry-Go-Round South Yorkshire coal trains serving Fiddlers Ferry Power Station. The line to Godley Junction is now a footpath.

Winter drag. In the days of electric loco-hauled passenger trains on the West Coast Mainline, diesel locos would drag them along sections of line when the overhead juice was turned off; this generally happened at weekend, to enable essential engineering work to be safely undertaken beneath the catenary. In the 1970s and early 1980s, the diesels of choice for this job tended to be Class 40s. In this rain-soaked photograph taken at Stockport on a Sunday during November 1980, an unidentified Class member is hauling a Manchester Piccadilly to London Euston Inter-City service. 86211 will resume haulage of the train at some point along the route, where the overhead wires became live, while the 40 would be detached and await the next northbound train. It would be coupled up and then dragged it to Manchester Piccadilly. The use of 40s in this way was popular with Class 40 bashers, these workings ensured plenty of extra track mileage behind what could be several class members in one day alone.

Within sight of Wilsons Brewery. The big building in the background is Wilsons Brewery and the location is Miles Platting station, neither of them exist today and little trace remains. Wilsons had lots of pubs in the Manchester area, but my mates and I didn't frequent many of them, favouring the city's other brewers' (Boddingtons, Chesters, Holts, Hydes) along with the plentiful Bass pubs. The brewery closed in 1987, while the large, well-appointed junction station closed in 1995 and was demolished soon afterwards. Part of the station awning was used at Ramsbottom station on the East Lancashire Railway. The Class 108 DMU is waiting for non-existent passengers prior to heading off into the rain. The next stop is Dean Lane, alongside Newton Heath Depot, on its journey to Rochdale, but the driver has forgotten to change the destination blind, it's only just left Manchester Victoria.

Heading for the Pennines. If someone ever said 'Show me a photograph of your favourite DMU, the Trans Pennine Class 124', this is probably not the one I'd produce. The 124 in this shot doesn't benefit from the unflattering and dull winter lighting. Miles Platting Junction has seen many hours of heavy rain – unsurprisingly, I was the only railway photographer on location there that winter's day in 1974. The signal man in the box probably had plenty of heat and was looking at me questioning my sanity. It was a great place to photograph trains being at the top of the steep Miles Platting Bank that climbs out of Manchester Victoria, and the vast array of semaphore signals and the vintage signal box were the icing on the cake. I like the grittiness of this photo. When I first saw it soon after receiving the prints I cast it to one side as a bad photo, now I think it's a terrific image packed with so much that is now long gone. The 124 is bound for Hull from Liverpool Lime Street; its next stop will be Stalybridge, then it will soon after bore through the Pennines (using the always damp Standedge Tunnel) and come out in Yorkshire.

Accentuated neglect. The poor weather has accentuated this scene of neglect at Bury Bolton Street, during January 1979. If the sun had been shining, it probably wouldn't have looked as bad. I reckon my photo wouldn't have been as good, though. Perhaps BR could have been excused a little for letting the station fall into rack and ruin? They were in the process of building Bury Interchange to replace Bolton Street. The 2x2 car sets of Class 504s, headed by M77165, will soon depart for Manchester Victoria. The platform I was standing on has now been transformed by the East Lancashire Railway, the transformation includes a building housing their highly popular Trackside pub. The other platforms and buildings have also been sympathetically restored, and the overall scene is a joy to behold, especially on running days, when it is full of DMUs, diesel and steam loco-hauled trains a-plenty. Plus, a group of enthusiasts are in the process of restoring the sole surviving 504 set in one of the railway's workshops. Once complete, it's intended to run on the line. It wouldn't be powered by a third rail electric supply though, another means of propulsion will be devised.

Returning empty. Until the 1980s, Manchester was the north of England's number one newspaper producer. They were printed at several locations in the centre of the city, quite close to Manchester Victoria and Piccadilly. Virtually all the national daily newspapers were produced on their presses, and they were distributed throughout the north and Scotland using long trains during the night. Most were loaded at Victoria's Platform 11. Once a train was loaded, it would depart, and then another would follow it in for loading. It was quite a slick operation. Open-backed motor trucks and vans shuttled between the presses and station, loaded to the gunnels with bundles of newspapers. Each one had a label stating which station along the way it should be offloaded at. From there another motor vehicle would pick them up for newsagents or a local distributer. Destinations of the trains included Barrow, Glasgow, Newcastle and Perth. During the morning and afternoon they'd return empty to Manchester or, in the case of those serving Victoria, they'd be stabled for a few hours at Red Bank Carriage Sidings. This shot, taken from the closed Manchester Exchange station, shows a Class 40 hauling empties to Red Bank. As you can see, it was pouring with rain that day. The disused station's roof did leak a little, but kept me largely dry for my November 1976 afternoon of photo taking.

Looking west. Not put off by the rain, one Saturday afternoon during November 1977, I motored east from my home in Denton to the Woodhead signal box. I had passed my driving test in Reddish a couple of months earlier, and I now had freedom of the Queen's highways, using my £100 H registration Ford Escort Mark 1 estate car. I could now go to otherwise inaccessible dream locations, Woodhead being one of them. The signal box was on the disused station, adjacent to Woodhead Tunnel's entrance and at the foot of a steep road leading off the A628. The signalman must have seen me park up as he seemed to be on standby, ready to invite me into his 1950s signal box. It was warm and dry, despite the metal single-glazed window frames. Unfortunately, being a Saturday afternoon, there were few trains booked to pass. This light engine move, a Class 76 pairing heading for Wath, was the only photo I took. You can see the signal box in the shot, as I had quickly stepped out of it to capture the scene on Kodak Tri-X film. After the loco had gone by, I said farewell to the signalman and got back in my car. I can't remember where I went next. Whilst a lot of the loco detail on this photo is lost in darkness, it does show how modern and well-cared for the permanent way was at Woodhead. This was typical of many parts of the route. Clearly no expense was being spared, in sharp contrast to those all too commonly neglected parts of 1970s British Rail. Just four years later, the whole route was closed.

Deltic atmosphere. This atmosphere-laden photograph was taken at York on 21 December 1980, the Sunday before Christmas. Deltic 55004 *Queen's Own Highlander* is waiting to depart with 1A06 the 11.43 York to Kings Cross. The semi-fast Inter-City trains to London were invariably hauled by a Class 55, this was as a result of being displaced by HSTs on the fast East Coast Mainline passenger workings. If funds were short and a Deltic-hauled run was desired, a one-stop run to Selby on a semi-fast was an affordable option. I did that several times. The Class 47 approaching York from the south is hauling a service from Liverpool Lime Street. At the time, these workings could often be hauled by a 40 or even a Class 55 – you can imagine the bashers' extreme disappointment when this 47 was used instead!

Dent at speed. Over the years preceding this photograph, I had seen lots of photographs taken on the Settle and Carlisle line. I had travelled along it several times, but never done any linesiding. Because the intermediate stations between Appleby and Settle were all closed, a car was really the only option if I wanted to take a few shots alongside the threatened-with-closure route. Of course, once I had passed my driving test the S&C went on my 'must do' list. It wasn't until May 1978 that I got to Dent station, one of my dream locations. My trusty Ford Escort never faltered and got me there just in time to take this photograph of 45029 racing through the (very wet) disused station with a Nottingham to Glasgow Central, via Dumfries, service. Like all the closed stations along the route, they are now open and kept in superb order – part of the station is now a holiday cottage.